Search for Immortality

Search for Immortality

By the Editors of Time-Life Books

TIME-LIFE BOOKS, ALEXANDRIA, VIRGINIA

CONTENTS

In Quest of Eternal Youth

Like the elderly women bathing at right in the mythical Fountain of Youth, most human beings yearn for eternal youth and health. If immortality itself is out of reach, many would gladly settle for a lesser, but still elusive, fate: to live for decades or centuries beyond the ordinary human span.

Hoping to extend their own lives, the medieval alchemists brewed elixirs of immortality—potions that supposedly allowed some of them to survive for hundreds of years. Chinese adepts of the same period relied in part on magical foods, such as peaches. Wealthy longevity seekers of many eras sought to postpone old age with various quasi-medical treatments, including the injection of youthful blood, with disappointing results.

In recent years, some scientists have put forward new and equally diverse proposals for added decades of active life. Certain gerontologists, for example, argue that lower body temperatures or reduced food intake could one day extend the human life span to a full 140 or even 200 years. Some visionary computer scientists have proposed a kind of mechanized afterlife in which human minds would be transferred, intact, into durable computerized memory. Meanwhile, on the fringes of the scientific community, others are taking aim at actual immortality. Proponents of so-called cryonic suspension have already preserved human bodies at −320 degrees Fahrenheit in hopes that their frozen "patients" can be revived centuries from now. By that time, they believe, medical technology may have indefinitely postponed human death.

Tired, aged women plunge into the rejuvenating waters of the Fountain of Youth in this sixteenth-century painting by Lucas Cranach the Younger. To the right of the pool, earlier bathers emerge young, beautiful, and ready for a banquet.

To Live Forever

ccording to the great yogi Paramahansa Yogananda, who introduced the West to many of India's mystical secrets, there lives high in the northern Himalayas a singular and illustrious guru. He has no fixed abode but moves from place to place in the mountains, accompanied by a small band of disciples—among them, according to Yogananda, two "highly advanced" American followers. Rarely seen by outsiders, the guru has been described as appearing no more than twenty-five years of age, with fair skin, dark, tender eyes, and lustrous, copper-colored hair. Despite his youthful visage, he is known as Babaji, which means "revered father." His real name is not known. Nor is the place or date of his birth. But these and other intriguing aspects of this mysterious master pale next to one salient element in Yogananda's description of him: Babaji is immortal.

Literally. Not just metaphorically immortal, like an individual of great achievement whose fame will survive the corporeal being, nor simply spiritually immortal in the sense of possessing an eternal soul: Babaji is said to be truly, physically immortal. "The secluded master," wrote Yogananda in his *Autobiography of a Yogi,* "has retained his physical form for centuries, perhaps millenniums." And he will continue to do so, explained Yogananda, as long as it helps him to serve his purpose as a spiritual teacher. That may be a very long time indeed, considering that Babaji's task is to inspire nations to give up war, materialism, and racial and religious hatred. Furthermore, Babaji's followers, too, are freed from the tyranny of death once they are accepted as his disciples.

Yogananda, a devout and respected spiritual leader who settled in America in the 1920s and founded the 150,000-member Self-Realization Fellowship, never claimed to have met Babaji himself. But he related to his followers and readers the experiences of other gurus whose veracity he trusted without question—among them his own primary mentor, Yukteswar, and a swami named Kebalananda, whom he identified as "my saintly Sanskrit tutor." Both these men were among several who told Yogananda of personal encounters with the deathless Babaji.

Kebalananda described experiences he had when traveling with Babaji's group in the Himalayas. It was he, in fact, who reported that two Americans were among the alleged immortals in the great guru's company. Kebalananda said that when the band had been in one place a while, Babaji would utter the words "Dera danda uthao"—"Let us lift our camp and staff," a reference to the bamboo staff he always carries. Often, the whole group would then be instantaneously transported by astral means to another mountain peak. On other occasions, the band would make the journey on foot.

Babaji, said Yukteswar, has achieved a spiritual state "beyond human comprehension." He has reached the level of a *paramukta,* an individual who is "supremely freed" from death. Most paramuktas, escaping from the wheel of reincarnation, never return to a physical body. One who does choose to return, as Babaji did in order to help mankind, is called an avatar. Babaji's high spiritual attainments give him the power to be seen and recognized only when he wishes. Because his incorruptible body needs no food, he eats only as a social courtesy. He casts no shadow and leaves no footprint on the ground. He usually speaks Hindi but is capable of conversing in any language.

Kebalananda told of a stranger who appeared in one of Babaji's nearly inaccessible mountain camps. The man implored Babaji to accept him as a disciple. When Babaji did not answer, the would-be acolyte pointed to the rocky chasm below: He would rather jump to his death, he said, than live without Babaji's guidance.

"Jump then," the guru replied calmly. "I cannot accept you in your present state of development."

To the horror of Babaji's disciples, the man immediately threw himself over the precipice. Babaji ordered his followers to retrieve the shattered body, on which he laid his hand.   The stranger

opened his eyes, arose, and prostrated himself before the revered guru. Now, Babaji told him, he was ready for discipleship. "You have courageously passed a difficult test. Death shall not touch you again; now you are one of our immortal flock."

Both Yukteswar and Kebalananda, using almost identical words, told Yogananda another tale about Babaji. This one was secondhand, related to them by their mutual teacher Lahiri Mahasaya, a noted nineteenth-century guru. In 1861 Mahasaya was a thirty-three-year-old accountant in an Indian government military engineering office when a telegram ordered him to a remote Himalayan location to help establish a new army post. On a walk in the countryside near his new assignment, Mahasaya encountered a handsome young man with copper-colored hair.

"I see my telegram took effect," the stranger said in English. When Mahasaya asked what he meant, the man explained that he had "silently suggested" to the mind of the accountant's superior that Mahasaya be transferred to this area. "When one feels his unity with mankind," the stranger said, "all minds become transmitting stations through which he can work at will."

Mahasaya remained bewildered until the youth tapped him gently on the forehead. "At his magnetic touch, a wondrous current swept through my brain, releasing the sweet seed-memories of my previous life," Mahasaya said. "I remember!" he shouted. He not only recognized the stranger as Babaji but instantly recalled that in a previous existence Babaji had been his beloved guru.

That night, Babaji displayed his astonishing powers by materializing a vast palace "of dazzling gold . . . set amid landscaped gardens, reflected in tranquil pools . . . intricately

Ambrosia and nectar, the food and drink of immortality, fuel the revels of Greek divinities in Raphael's Marriage of Cupid (above). Such meals ensured that the gods would never die.

inlaid with great diamonds, sapphires and emeralds. Men of angelic countenance were stationed by gates redly resplendent with rubies." The palace was no mere vision; Mahasaya ran his hands over the walls, held and examined a jeweled vase, and smelled incense and roses. He ate litchis and curry from a bowl that was empty until he reached for it. One of the guru's disciples explained that Babaji "created this beautiful mansion out of his mind and is holding its atoms together by the power of his will."

Babaji spent the next ten days initiating Lahiri Mahasaya into the secrets of kriya-yoga, a meditative technique for withdrawing life energies from the outer senses to achieve understanding of the spiritual reality within. Then he sent Mahasaya back to his home and family, instructing him to spend his life bringing the spiritual values of kriya-yoga to people like himself, whose domestic obligations and encumbrances made pure asceticism difficult or impossible. A few days later, Mahasaya could not resist telling some friends of his experience in the mountains. "Lahiri," one said gently, "your mind has been under a strain." The others nodded agreement. Mahasaya responded rashly: "If I call him, my guru will appear right in this house."

He immediately regretted his claim, but "the group was eager to behold such a phenomenon." Mahasaya told them to wait outside the room, closed the door behind them, and "sank into the meditative state, humbly summoning my guru." Babaji soon materialized, but he was displeased. "Do you call me for a trifle?" he asked sternly. "Truth is for earnest seekers, not for those of idle curiosity."

He agreed to stay, however, so Mahasaya would not be discredited before his friends. When the door—the only entrance to the room—was thrown open, the doubters were amazed to find Mahasaya was now inexplicably accompanied by a young stranger with copper hair and glowing skin, sitting cross-legged on the floor.

Thus it was that the ancient but ever-youthful guru shared a bowl of *halua,* a farina-based porridge similar to today's Cream of Wheat, with seven middle-class Indian professionals and businessmen in the city of Moradabad in 1861. Babaji invited the men to touch him to see for themselves that he was real. "Doubts dispelled, my friends prostrated themselves on the floor in awed repentance," Mahasaya reported. After the meal, Babaji blessed each of them. Then a brilliant flash suddenly filled the room as the guru disappeared into a "spreading vaporous light," and

"trillions of tiny . . . sparks faded into the infinite reservoir."

Despite such tales of his spectacular yogic power, it is Babaji's reputed ability to live forever and to confer immortality on others that makes him an irresistibly intriguing figure to most who hear or read of him, especially in the West. Reports of people who never die—or who live what seem impossibly long lives—always compel attention.

Immortality, apparently, is not all that uncommon in popular Indian belief. Yogananda mentioned another avatar, Agastya, who was famed in southern India where he "worked many miracles during the centuries preceding and following the Christian era, and is credited with retaining his physical form even to this day." In the 1930s an English journalist in Bombay described a yogi called the Ant Teacher (because he fed ants from a bag of rice powder), who was said to be some 400 years old. He reportedly attained this remarkable age by exerting his will to draw life force up his spine and push it into a tiny hole in his brain, where, he said, his soul resided.

Rumors of immortality have long had currency in the Western world as well. The self-titled Comte de Saint-Germain, an alchemist probably born in the early 1700s, claimed to be old enough to have been personally acquainted with Solomon and Sheba and allegedly has been sighted, still alive and well, in the twentieth century. Another alchemist, Nicholas Flamel, born about 1330, was reported to be still alive as late as 1818—although according to other accounts, he was actually last seen in 1761. Resurrection has its attractions, too: Ancient Spell Raises the Dead! screamed the bold-faced headline over a recent tabloid report that doctors at a (conveniently) remote Chinese university used old Tibetan ointments and chants to briefly revive a woman dead of a heart infection.

nd now, as the Cryonics Society of New York has made graphically clear in an advertisement that promotes its deep-freeze body-preservation program, the notion is abroad that anyone who can afford it may have a very real chance to live forever. ''An Invitation to Help Attain Physical Immortality: You will have a unique opportunity to work for the attainment of the most profound objective imaginable—the indefinite extension of your life,'' the society declared. The society's ultimate goal, the ad stated unequivocally, is ''biological immortality—a life of youthful vigor untempered by physical limitations.''

Clearly, humankind's obsession with the whole subject of defying death and defeating the ravages of age is a case of hope springing eternal—a hope some say is totally unwarranted while others, including more than a few with scientific credentials, are not so sure. Blessed and cursed with the ability to remember the past and imagine the future, people from the earliest cultures to the present have nourished a deep yearning to be like gods, to stop or at least significantly slow down the clock of bodily deterioration

that ticks inexorably toward the moment of demise. ''The desire to be physically immortal,'' wrote physician and gerontologist Roy L. Walford, ''or at least to live much longer and in full health, has been humanity's oldest dream.''

The dream has expressed itself in many forms. Most societies have honored their longest-lived individuals, commemorating them in myth or Holy Writ, hailing their annual milestones with telegrams from the monarch or the broadcast congratulations of a television weatherman. Every culture has cherished practices and arts perceived to offer the possibility of immortality or very long life. Mental and spiritual regimens, elixirs, black magic, diets, arcane sexual practices, and exacting laboratory procedures have all been enlisted in the campaign to hold death at bay.

Modern researchers the world over are pursuing the age-old quest with more urgency than ever. Like alchemists of old, hunched over their retorts hoping to uncover the elixir of life, scientists of today are seeking dramatic and exotic means to extend that immutable span. In laboratories around the globe, experimenters in cryonics, cloning, cell regeneration, genetic engineering, severely reduced nutrition, bionics, and robotics search diligently for new clues to the secrets of long life and eternal youth.

In their efforts they join a long parade of philosophers and kings, charlatans, priests, alchemists, adventurers, poets, and earlier scientists who have eagerly taken up the cause of extending human life beyond its normally alloted limits. Yet despite this universal preoccupation with the theme, one of its enduring mysteries is that nobody has ever been sure just what those life limits are.

This much is certain: If the words of the Bible are accepted at face value, people used to live a lot longer than they do now. The Book of Genesis in the Old Testament tells of Adam and six of his direct descendants who each lived more than 900 years. Most notable was Methuselah, whose age at death is recorded as 969. At the age of 187, Methuselah sired a son, Lamech, the first of his several sons and daughters. Lamech, who died at 777, was in turn the father of Noah, the last of the 900-plus oldsters. Noah rode out the Flood in his ark at age 600 and lived on for another 350 years thereafter.

Many of Noah's descendants also are said to have lived for hundreds of years, although their life spans decreased steadily. Moses, just a few generations later, lived only 120 years, which seems to confirm Genesis's final bulletin on the human life span. "My spirit shall not abide in man forever," said God, according to the Scripture, "for he is flesh, but his days shall be a hundred and twenty years."

While many contend that those accounts of multiple-century life spans are either mythical or errors in translation, perhaps resulting from a different method of measuring time back then, some people with strong religious beliefs accept the Bible's report on Methuselah and his long-lived cohorts as the literal truth. The dwindling of life span in the generations after Noah is taken to indicate the growing distance between humankind and the Creator: Having fallen increasingly out of favor through moral error, humanity lost the privilege of long life.

There are others, moreover, who accept the biblical accounts of longevity as true for reasons that have nothing to do with religion. "A dozen or so years ago I would have been inclined to regard these stories of fabulous life spans as ridiculous," wrote C. Edward Burtis, one author who delved into the subject. "Today I am not so sure." He notes that the disparity between Methuselah's 969 years and Moses' 120 makes it unlikely that a different scale for reckoning time—which would apply equally in both cases—could explain Methuselah's great age. He suggests there must have been some other factor that over time worked to decrease longevity, including changes in farming methods and not consuming the right minerals. "The key, the most significant key," said Burtis, is "the steady decline in the life spans from the earliest recordings."

In the 1950s the same pattern was noticed by a physician and nutritionist named Daniel Colin Munro, who associated the decline with what he deduced from biblical references to be a general dietary trend. Starting with Adam, he said, humans gradually went from eating raw meat to cooked meat to vegetables to grains, and their lives apparently shortened as a result—a puzzling conclusion indeed in view of today's medical judgments about the relative effects of meat and grain on health and longevity.

The Old Testament is but one of many sources that relate accounts of extreme longevity. Ancient Sanskrit texts include many stories of humans whose lives reached far beyond the normal span. A notable example is King Yayati, a deeply religious man whose virtuous conduct freed him—as well as his subjects—from the ills of old age and disease. Yayati and his people all were destined to look no older than age twenty-five forever. But envious old Yama, the god of death, was jealous of this earthly bastion of immortality and complained to Indra, the god of rain and thunder, about Yayati's parallel heaven. So Indra sent old age, in the form of a beautiful woman, to tempt Yayati. Beguiled by the temptress's charm and sweet songs, the king began to neglect his religious duties—and he began to age. When Yayati finally yielded to his fate after years of struggle, his subjects decided they did not want to live without him and chose to accompany him to heaven.

Another cherished Hindu myth describes the long-lived Uttarakuru, a race who dwelt in the mountains of northern India. Their lives were blessed by a magic tree, whose fruit protected the Uttarakuru from illness and old age and extended their life span to a thousand years. The sacred tree as a symbol of long life or immortality is integral to many cultures. Adam and Eve, of course, might also have achieved godlike longevity from Eden's Tree of Life had they not gotten themselves thrown out of the Garden. (As it was, Adam made it to the age of 930, according to Genesis.)

Even leaving aside for the moment alchemists who supposedly achieved immortality by means of their concoctions, there have been over more recent centuries a number of breathtaking claims of great age, although most of them were characterized by an absence of any substantial proof.

For example, the Countess of Desmond, an Irish noblewoman who died in 1604, was said to have been 140 years of age at her death (some put her at 145 years). One writer said she was well known for her love of dancing "even when a hundred Christmasses had passed over her head." He added the much more astonishing information that when she was 140 she walked all the way from Bristol to London, more than 120 miles, to seek relief at court from her impoverished state. In his *History of the World,* Sir Walter Raleigh claimed he knew the old countess himself, and that she had married in the 1460s—which would mean, if she was actually 140 in 1604, that she had been wed not long after her birth. As a later author circumspectly put it, Raleigh was "not regarded as a paragon of veracity."

A Yorkshire fisherman by the name of Henry Jenkins said that he was 169 as he neared his death in 1670. When he had made a sworn statement in court three years earlier, however, his age was declared to be 157, which would have made him 160 when he died. That would be impressive enough, but there is no indication the court required proof of his age. Jenkins claimed to remember boyhood experiences involving the battle of Flodden Field between the English and the Scots in 1513.

A Scandinavian sailor named Christian Jacob Drackenburg was accepted by newspapers as being 149 when he died in 1772; they called him the Old Man of the North. He said he married at the age of 111, and at the end of his life he was still walking four miles at a stretch—but he never produced evidence of his date of birth.

One of the most widely accepted claims of unusual longevity was that of Thomas Parr, a Shropshireman who alleged himself to be 152 in the year 1635. A peculiar chain of events lent credence to his story, not only with the public but among scientific men of the era. One of Charles I's court favorites, Thomas, Earl of Arundel and Surrey, was visiting some of his estates in Shropshire when he heard of Old Parr and went to see the aged peasant. Thomas at once decided the king would find Parr an amusing curiosity, so he loaded the old man onto a horse-drawn litter and took him to London. Parr became a court sensation and the talk of the town. But the trip must have taken its toll, because the peasant sickened and died in November 1635.

The story does not end there, however. The king's favorite doctor was none other than William Harvey, who was already famous and highly respected throughout Europe's scientific com-

M. LE COMTE DE SAINT GERMAIN
Lieutenant Général des Armées du Roi
Com.dr de l'Ordre R.al et Milit.re de S.t Louis
Secretaire d'État au Département de la Guerre.

Most stories about the mysterious Comte de Saint-Germain (left) suggest he died in 1784 at the age of 188—or, in one tale, a ripe old 223—and was duly buried in France. According to other accounts, however, the venerable nobleman subsequently reappeared and remains alive and active today.

14

Thomas Parr
The Old Man of Shropshire

Published by Edr.ᵈ Evans, 1, Great Queen Street, Lincoln's Inn Fields.

munity for being the first to show how blood circulated through the body. King Charles asked the physician to perform an autopsy on Thomas Parr. In his Latin notes on his findings, Dr. Harvey marveled over Parr's fine physical condition. The "body was muscular," the heart was "healthy," and the bones were "not at all brittle." Even the hair on Parr's arms was still black, he noted.

Harvey never gave the impression that he thought this excellent condition could mean Parr was not really as old as alleged. The physician's apparent acceptance of the peasant's claim caused other scientists and scholars throughout Europe to also accept it as true. Some continued to hold this view right up into the twentieth century, even though Harvey's critics pointed out that the physician was an accomplished courtier who would not have wanted to expose the king's gullibility nor to offend a powerful nobleman like the Earl of Arundel.

The twentieth century, too, has produced its share of claimants to more years than scientific authorities believe possible—and convincing proof is as scarce as ever. On May 6, 1933, for instance, a London paper proclaimed that the "oldest man on earth" had just died in China. His year of birth was given as 1680. In his supposed 253 years, he had outlived twenty-three wives; a twenty-fourth, his 64-year-old widow, survived him.

At about the same time there came to public attention a case that at the very least made greater pretense to legitimacy, and which many people accepted as genuine. The individual involved was Zaro Agha, a Turk, who said he was born in 1774. The unusual element here was that in 1930 the Turkish government issued Agha a passport officially confirming his age to be 156. Agha claimed that as a young man he had seen Napoleon leading his troops into Syria in 1799. Such stories made highly readable articles for the many newspapers who sent correspondents to interview Agha—including the *Times* of London, which probably had more prestige and a greater reputation for probity than any other major journal of the era. An impresario signed up

Hindu worshipers crowd the shallows of the Ganges to bathe in, drink, and carry away the revered waters. Pole-and-rope barriers help to ensure safety, and boats stand ready to ferry the faithful to the Sangam, the holy point where the Yamuna and the Ganges rivers meet.

With a serpent as their churning rope and a mountain as a paddle, Hindu gods (left) and demons (right) churn the ocean to obtain amrita, the nectar of life, in this eighteenth-century Indian painting. The helpful tortoise is Vishnu.

Crowding the Waters of Life

On February 6, 1989, some 22 million Hindus thronged the shores of the Ganges and the Yamuna rivers where those two sacred streams meet at Allahabad, in northern India. The people had all come in search of the same reward: eternal life. The crowd is believed to have been the largest ever in one place at one time, and over the next forty-nine days another 38 million or so showed up—such is the compelling attraction of immortality.

The eternal life they sought was spiritual, however, not physical. As Hindus, they hoped to escape the ever-turning wheel of repeated corporeal incarnations and achieve the flesh-free peace of nirvana. Hindus believe there is no better occasion for securing this release than the Kumbha Mela, or

Festival of the Pottery Jar. According to their scriptures, gods and demons working together in the ancient past *(above)* churned from the ocean the nectar of eternal life, called amrita. But after collecting it in a pottery jar, the Golden Kumbha, the factions fought over it and in their struggle spilled four drops. One drop each fell on Ujjain, Hardwar, Nasik, and Allahabad, and now the festival is held every three years at one of those four holy cities.

The 1989 Kumbha Mela at Allahabad was deemed especially auspicious because it coincided with a lunar eclipse and an alignment of the Sun, the Moon, and Jupiter that occurs only every 144 years. Enhancing this sacred time was the venerableness of the location. The Ganges is Hinduism's

A bearded holy man, or sadhu, bearing the clay-paste marks of his sect on his forehead, holds out the brass pot in which he collects sacred Ganges water. His vessel is a symbol of the Golden Kumbha, the pottery vase that Hindu scriptures say contained the nectar amrita.

most honored river, and the holiest place for bathing is at the point of land called the Sangam, where the Ganges and Yamuna converge. Here a third river is said to join the other two—the Saraswati, the invisible river of enlightenment. Hindus believe that immersion in the Ganges near where the amrita fell, and during the Kumbha Mela, guarantees release from the earthly cycle of death and rebirth.

Although all of Hinduism's many sects and doctrines are represented and welcome at the Kumbha Mela, it is the sadhus, or holy men, who lead the proceedings and give the event its spiritual depth. Most revered of sadhus

Riding on a float, a celebrant blows twin trumpets to announce the procession of the nagas—most revered of the sadhus—to the water. Attendees making way for the nagas throw rice in the air to greet the holy men as they pass.

Garlanded in beads and mari-golds, the sadhu seated at center has covered his face in ashes. Sadhus and gurus, with their followers, are granted their own special encampments at the Kumbha Mela festivals.

A militant mounted naga, clad in cow-dung ashes and mari-gold garlands, helps lead the procession to the river for the first day's bathing. In keeping with the rider's high station, his horse is elaborately decorated.

First to bathe in the early-morning darkness of the first and most auspicious feast day, several naked nagas (left) wash the cow-dung ashes from their bodies in the cold water at the Sangam. Hindus believe that these holy men's ablutions further sanctify the waters for bathers who come after them.

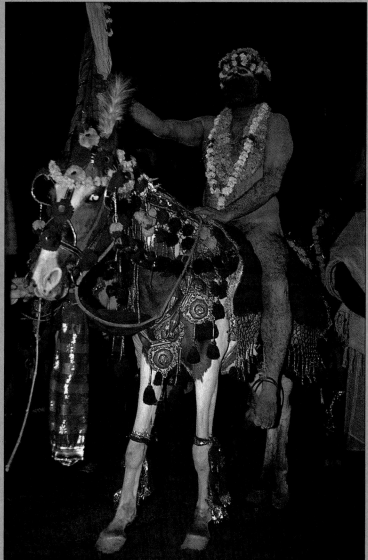

Shaded by ornate parasols, gurus of high rank are borne by their devotees toward the holy waters as the spectacular procession continues. Bright placards called patakas (top) identify the various sects attending.

are the nagas, ascetic practitioners of rigorous martial and spiritual disciplines. Nagas lead the first procession to the river, to bathe at the Sangam at the astrologically most favorable moment. Devout Hindus line the procession route, straining to touch the holy men and smearing their own foreheads with the dust nagas have trod.

Celebrants of the 1989 festival began arriving at the river in early January, occupying a government-built 3,600-acre tent city with roads, water, and power lines. On every day of the fifty-day ritual, worshipers stood in the chilly waters of the winter Ganges amid a devotional din of chiming bells. They chanted mantras, pouring offerings of milk into the river and setting adrift tiny boats of stitched leaves bearing flowers and sweets, in thanks for their newfound immortality.

A worshiper drenches herself from toes to scalp in the Ganges. Many celebrants can be heard chanting a Hindu prayer to the Seven Sacred Rivers: "O, Ganges! O, Yamuna! O, Godavari! O, Saraswati! O, Narmada, Sindhu, Kaveri! May you all be pleased to be manifest in these waters!"

Women work together to dry a billowing sari in the wind on the riverbank (below), after washing it in a traditional Kumbha Mela purification rite. Although women are all but excluded from Hinduism's highest spiritual aspirations, many do attend the Kumbha festivals.

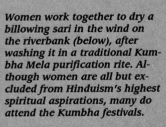

Agha and took the former porter and his precious passport on a profitable tour of the world—including the United States, where the curious flocked to see someone born before the American Revolution. Agha went home to Turkey in 1933 and died not long thereafter.

All these examples are generally discounted by modern authorities on aging, who instead look at the past and see a human life span that has increased for clear reasons and that has never reached the years claimed by people like Zaro Agha. It is believed that at first the life span of proto-humans increased through evolution. This notion is based on the observation that among mammals the greater the brain weight in proportion to the body weight the longer lived is the animal. Fossils show that early hominids had much smaller brains for their body sizes than do modern humans; thus it is thought that their life spans were much shorter. Hominid brain weights grew rapidly until about 100,000 years ago, so it is presumed that longevity increased accordingly and reached a plateau at about that time. It appears that the brain-to-body ratio has not changed since then, although no one can say for certain there has not been some growth in, say, the last 10,000 years, because the increase could be too small to measure.

Life spans, of course, have increased remarkably during historical times even without any help from evolution. Historians have determined that citizens of Rome during the early years of the Christian era, when the Roman Empire flourished, lived a mere twenty-two years, on average. Many Romans lived far longer, but infant mortality and infectious diseases were cruel oddsmakers in those days, and the low probability of a long life was strongly biased by the multitudes who died in childhood. By the beginning of the twentieth century—almost 2,000 years later—better living conditions, disease control, and medical care had added two to three decades to the average life span. In less than a century after that, improvements in sanitation and nutrition combined with modern medicine to extend life expectancy another twenty to thirty years—for those lucky enough to live in highly developed nations. People in these favored cultures now survive to an average age of more than seven decades. In many underdeveloped countries, by contrast, death still comes much sooner. Present-day inhabitants of such nations as Ethiopia, Somalia, and Bangladesh, often ravaged by famine, disease, and war, tend to be cut off in their forties or early fifties—no better odds of long life than were enjoyed by late-nineteenth-century Europeans.

These statistical outlines of life expectancy deal with the actual length of time the average person in a given society can expect to live. Important as these figures are to governments, insurance companies, product advertisers, and demographers, they do not address the issue of human potential. The puzzle remains: Pestilence and violence aside, what is the longest a human can live?

Some gerontologists, scientists who study aging and the problems of the aged, think they have an answer. Based not only on biological research but also on the work of anthropologists and sociologists among long-lived human societies, they estimate that the maximum human life span is between 110 and 120 years. By this age, they contend, the body simply wears out, even if it has survived all the mishaps, diseases, and flawed genes that normally claim most lives decades earlier. Furthermore, according to most gerontologists, despite the multitudes of experiments tried over the centuries and all the medical marvels of the last hundred years, this ultimate human term probably has not been lengthened by a twinkling since modern humans replaced earlier hominids on the evolutionary scene.

But some authorities say those limits are not necessarily permanent. "On an evolutionary scale, the human life span has increased," notes Leonard Hayflick, director of the University of Florida's Center for Gerontological Studies. "This fact is important because it implies that the human life span, even if it has been fixed for millennia, has the potential to increase in the future."

Caleb E. Finch, professor of gerontology at the University of Southern California in Los Angeles, and Robert M.

Sapolsky, a Stanford University biologist, point out that some species do not age, or senesce, as science terms it. "Startlingly enough," the pair reported in a collaborative article, "for many species things are otherwise. Bristlecone pine trees and rockfish, certain parameciums and some social insect queens, to name just a few, do not senesce."

ecause their cells do not wear out, individuals in those species would live virtually forever were they not eventually eliminated by an outside force, such as a predator or drought. In fact, what is believed to be the world's oldest living tree, a bristlecone pine in the Sierra Nevada in the southwestern United States, has survived for some 4,600 years. In some insect species, a nonsenescing queen who uses up all the sperm she took in during her once-ever mating is deliberately killed by the workers who up till then have devoted their lives to feeding and protecting her. Otherwise, she would linger on indefinitely, an unproductive burden to the colony, because old age itself would never do her in. Interestingly, it appears that nonsenescence was the original way of life on earth, since nonaging species in general are less complex and seem to have evolved earlier than species that do age, such as mammalian species. Obviously, it could be of great interest and importance to human beings to discover exactly why those species never age.

Some people believe the answer to extending life is not to be found in the physical realm of science at all. They insist that spiritual enlightenment is the force that can stretch the sullen bonds of the flesh into dimensions beyond medical expectation. Such claims are difficult to test, but some studies of meditation's effects on health and longevity have yielded surprising results. A 1982 survey showed that—diet and chronological age being equal—people who had been regularly meditating for years tested as "biologically younger" than subjects who had been meditating over a shorter span, and the latter in turn were biologically younger than a control group that did not meditate at all.

A 1989 report on a study by five Harvard scholars actually concluded that Transcendental Meditation, as taught by the Maharishi Mahesh Yogi, could "literally extend human life." Seventy-three residents of eight nursing homes—their average age was eighty-one—were randomly assigned to several groups. One group was coached in TM, others were trained in different kinds of mental control and relaxation procedures, and some received no treatment at all. After three years, 100 percent of the TM subjects were still alive. The other categories had significantly lower survival rates—only 77.3 percent for the untreated group.

Whether more knowledge of evolution or nonsenescent species, or of yoga, meditation, or any metaphysical practice, will ever add a day to the human life span is still an open question. But it is a good guess that people will continue seeking ways to live longer, just as they have since the awakening of humanity.

Anthropologists who dig into paleolithic campsites know that there was nothing permanent about the settlements of people who wandered the earth in those days—except for the graves. However changeable their own existences, they were at pains to see their dead comfortably settled as if waiting to be awakened for another life: in mounds of earth heaped for the purpose, in caves, or beneath piles of stones apparently constructed to permanently mark the burial site. "The city of the dead," wrote social critic and historian Lewis Mumford, "antedates the city of the living."

As humankind settled down, the concern for seeing the dead off in style increased. "The oldest, most numerous, and most imposing relics of our ancestors are funerary," noted English historian Arnold Toynbee. Almost all ancient peoples believed in some form of afterlife, but in a sense the Egyptians sought physical immortality; they thought a satisfactory life after death was obtainable only if the body was preserved. That was why they buried the corpses of poor villagers in dry sand that forestalled deterioration, and mummified their pharaohs with elaborate ceremony and tucked them safely away in gigantic stone pyramidal tombs.

Nowadays, some modern occultists and paranormal

In search of a New World fountain of youth, sixteenth-century Spanish explorer Juan Ponce de León (standing, lower right) pauses with his men beside a promising stream in this nineteenth-century engraving. Ponce de León explored Bimini, Florida, and the Yucatán in his fruitless quest for immortality.

theorists view the pyramids as more than just funereal safe-deposit boxes. Pyramid enthusiasts believe the forms emit various kinds of energy rays with life-enhancing power. They say ancient Egyptians employed these rays to preserve bodies by preventing decay. The body in turn would "broadcast the energy to the soul" to guard the soul against death. Modern promoters of pyramid power sell a number of pyramid-style contraptions that supposedly concentrate the "life force," and thus—by implication, although legal caution may preclude outright claims—extend life.

A notion that first gripped the human imagination eons ago is that of a water source that confers immortality, or at least a long and youthful life, on anyone who drinks from it—or, in some cases, bathes in it. The Greek historian Herodotus, famed for his accounts of the Greco-Persian wars, wrote in the fifth century BC of a Persian king whose spies reported a spring of magical water in Ethiopia. The water rejuvenated those who drank it, enabling some to live to 120 years. Herodotus accepted the tale, passing it along whole to his readers, who in turn apparently readily believed that youth could be regained so easily.

The idea of a fountain of youth proved one of the most alluring and enduring of human dreams. Its best-known adherent was probably a Spanish governor of Puerto Rico named Juan Ponce de León, who in 1513 set out to track down the rumored fountain in the unexplored reaches of the New World. As it turned out, however, he found death instead of youth, suffering a mortal wound in an Indian attack in Florida in 1521.

While the fountain eluded Ponce de León, millions of latter-day sybarites have discovered real-life substitutes in a variety of healing waters. European spas of the nineteenth century drew many patrons who believed the waters would lift the burdens of old age. Early Europeans treated these outpourings of mineral waters as holy wells or springs, where prayers were offered and healing received. The hot springs at Bath, England, are typical; they were used by the Celts and then by the Romans almost two millennia ago and remain the center of a thriving tourist industry today.

Another example of antiquity's interest in immortality was noted by Galen, a second-century-AD Greek physician. Galen first gained attention as a sports doctor, patching up wounded gladiators at Pergamum, and rose to be physician to Emperor Commodus in Rome, where he had the time and facilities to win his historical reputation as the founder of experimental physiology. In one of his many treatises, Galen described a book by a colleague who claimed to be able to prevent old age. The unnamed doctor said he could provide immortality to those who came to him when still young and stayed under his care from then on. Neither the book nor any descriptions of its supposed life-extension methods are known to have survived.

Of course, for as long as it has been the object of earnest quests, immortality, or the promise of it, has also figured in scams of one kind or another. Venetian traveler Marco Polo learned of an especially ingenious one while crossing Persia on his thirteenth-century journey to China. A local ruler created a virtual paradise in an isolated and secret valley. There, palaces filled with silk-covered furniture and ornamented with gold were surrounded, Polo said, by a "luxurious garden, stored with every delicious fruit and every fragrant shrub." Through a network of conduits, "streams of wine, milk, honey and . . . pure water" flowed throughout the garden and buildings. And finally, the ruler peopled his secret valley solely with "elegant and beautiful damsels, accomplished in the arts of singing . . . dancing, and especially those of dalliance and amorous allurement."

The whole place was sealed off from the rest of the ruler's territory by an impregnable fortress built across the valley's narrow entrance. From time to time, Polo wrote, the chief summoned to his court certain courageous boys and young men, between the ages of twelve and twenty, to train for service in his guard. Each day he would remind them of the prophet Muhammad's promise of paradise to the faithful who obeyed the laws of Islam. Well, said the ruler to his young charges, he, too, "had the power of ad-

mitting to Paradise such as he should choose to favor." After some days of this, he would have them drugged with opium and carried off through secret passageways into his hidden garden of delights.

There the lads awakened in a sumptuous place literally running with milk, honey, and wine; they were surrounded by beautiful women who obliged their every fantasy until, "intoxicated with excess of enjoyment," they believed themselves "assuredly in Paradise." After four or five days, they were drugged again and returned to court. There they declared they had been to paradise, courtesy of their ruler, who assured them that if they remained loyal and fought selflessly in his defense, they would on their earthly deaths return to that place for eternity. As a consequence, said Marco Polo, the chief was served by a fierce and fiercely loyal band of "disciplined assassins, none of whom felt terror at the risk of losing their own lives."

The themes of eternal youth and immortality have always been entwined. No one ever wanted the gift of eternal life without the vitality to enjoy it. Many instructive myths demonstrate the concern. One Icelandic saga, for instance, tells of a mortal being who shed his skin every twenty years, a rejuvenation rite that not only made him immortal but also restored him each time to the prime age of thirty years. The Greek myth of Tithonus also makes the point vividly. Eos, goddess of dawn, pleaded with Zeus to grant immortality to her human lover, Tithonus. But she forgot to include eternal youth in her wish, and literal-minded Zeus granted only what she asked. So Tithonus never died but grew more and more decrepit as he aged, until at last Eos had to shut him in a room—where, presumably, he still lies, babbling and cursing his immortality.

In *Gulliver's Travels,* satirist Jonathan Swift presents the "Struldbrugs," people who never die but who keep aging. Eventually, the Struldbrugs "find themselves cut off from all possibility of pleasure; and whenever they see a funeral they lament that others have gone to a harbour of rest to which they themselves can never hope to arrive."

Another case in which immortality functioned as curse rather than boon is that of the Flying Dutchman, a tale that many times has crossed the line from legend to seeming fact and back again. The basic story involves a Dutch sea captain whose behavior toward his passengers and crew during a storm was so brutal that he was condemned by God to sail through the gale forever. Not only must he live eternally with his own iniquity, but he also is doomed to strike terror in and bring misfortune to any voyagers unlucky enough to meet his ghost ship on the high seas.

As a legend, the Dutchman has provided a dramatic structure for stories, poems, and a famous opera. But the undying captain and his ship apparently refuse to stay in fiction. For centuries, sailors the world over have claimed they saw the vessel. Probably most notable was a close view reported in June 1881 by the future King George V of England, his brother Prince Albert Victor, and thirteen crewmen of their Royal Navy training ship. The apparition was bathed in "a strange red light, as of a phantom ship all aglow." Admiral Karl Dönitz, commander of the German navy in World War II, said he saw the fearful ship when on a tour of duty in Far Eastern waters.

Possible negative aspects of immortality, however, seem never to have gained the upper hand

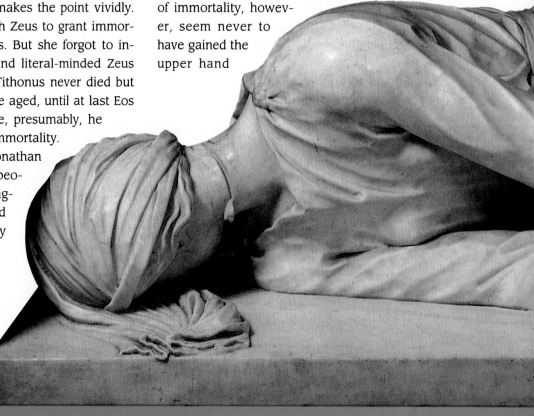

Her face covered with a burial cloth, the early Christian martyr Saint Cecilia lies dead of deep neck wounds in this seventeenth-century statue by Carlo Maderna. Tradition holds that Maderna modeled the statue after the saint's own body when it was disinterred, miraculously preserved, fourteen centuries after her death.

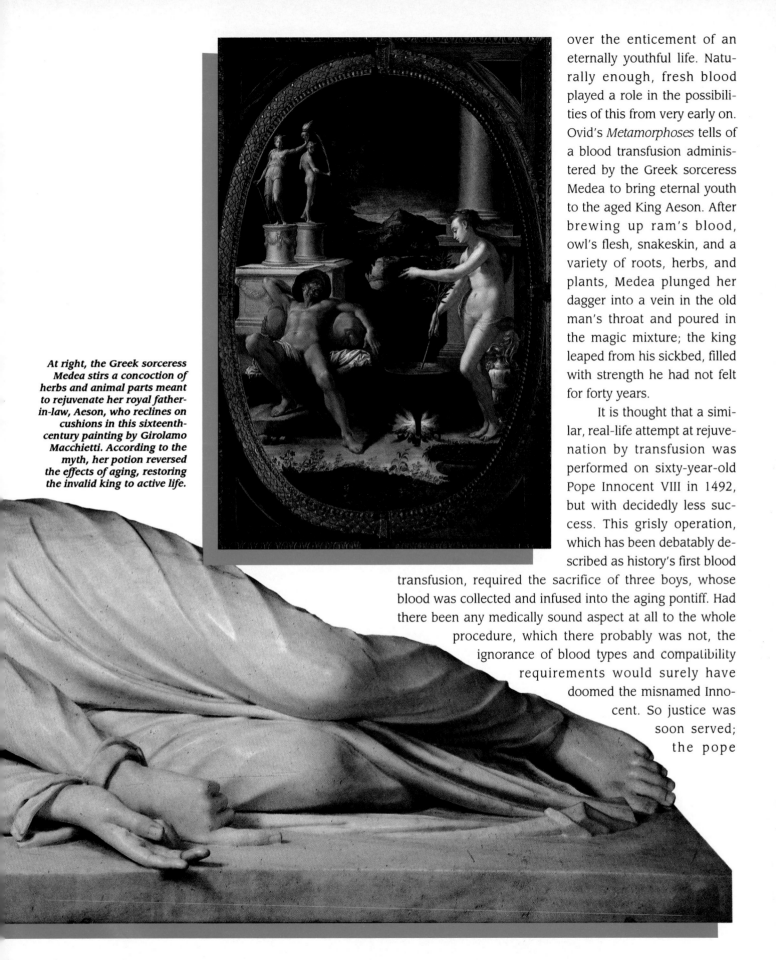

over the enticement of an eternally youthful life. Naturally enough, fresh blood played a role in the possibilities of this from very early on. Ovid's *Metamorphoses* tells of a blood transfusion administered by the Greek sorceress Medea to bring eternal youth to the aged King Aeson. After brewing up ram's blood, owl's flesh, snakeskin, and a variety of roots, herbs, and plants, Medea plunged her dagger into a vein in the old man's throat and poured in the magic mixture; the king leaped from his sickbed, filled with strength he had not felt for forty years.

It is thought that a similar, real-life attempt at rejuvenation by transfusion was performed on sixty-year-old Pope Innocent VIII in 1492, but with decidedly less success. This grisly operation, which has been debatably described as history's first blood transfusion, required the sacrifice of three boys, whose blood was collected and infused into the aging pontiff. Had there been any medically sound aspect at all to the whole procedure, which there probably was not, the ignorance of blood types and compatibility requirements would surely have doomed the misnamed Innocent. So justice was soon served; the pope

At right, the Greek sorceress Medea stirs a concoction of herbs and animal parts meant to rejuvenate her royal father-in-law, Aeson, who reclines on cushions in this sixteenth-century painting by Girolamo Macchietti. According to the myth, her potion reversed the effects of aging, restoring the invalid king to active life.

In an engraving (left) from the Kneipp cure handbook, women receive gushes of water on the knee and head. Kneipp called this treatment "the feet's best friend, as it lures and entices the reluctant blood down into the imperfectly filled veins."

A picture of the men's treatment room (right) illustrates, from left to right, Kneipp's "lightning gush," "knee gush," and "upper-body gush."

Below, villagers make Kneipp's water cure part of an outing in 1908. "How must the poor feet rejoice," Kneipp wrote of barefoot wading, "to come out at last from their cages."

Der Blitzguß. Der Knieguß. Der Oberguß.

Die Kneippkur.

A Priest's Peculiar Cure

Late in the nineteenth century, thousands of Europeans eager to live longer, healthier lives flocked to the Bavarian village of Wörishofen, site of the famous "Kneipp cure." Developed by the town priest, Father Sebastian Kneipp (right), the cold-water cure was based on a regimen that the pastor credited with saving his own life.

As an impoverished seminary student, Kneipp said, he had fallen victim to a mysterious "steadily increasing disease" that doctors could not cure. The young man had already resigned himself to an early death when he happened to read a treatise on the curative powers of cold water. Following the little book's vigorous prescriptions, Kneipp bathed in brooks and rivers in all seasons and gradually regained his health. Water, he later declared, became his "best friend."

Over years, Father Kneipp refined that original treatment into a variety of rejuvenating procedures, some of them illustrated at left. To increase general health and vitality, the priest recommended whole-body immersions in water, "the colder the better," as well as barefoot walks on wet stones, in wet grass, in streams, and in snow. Treatment for specific ailments involved so-called gushes of water, which were directed over the torso, limbs, or head in precise patterns for exact periods of time. To keep cures affordable, gushes were administered with watering cans and garden hoses.

In 1897, after a lifetime devoted to his water remedies, the once sickly pastor died at the age of seventy-six. Many of his methods still remain in use at European spas.

Clothed in his accustomed clerical garb, Sebastian Kneipp was probably in his seventies when this photograph was taken. Among those persons said to be revitalized by Kneipp's water cure was the well-known financier Nathaniel Rothschild.

died not long after the travesty. His secular effort to extend his life must have represented a failure of spirit; it certainly ran counter to the tradition in many cultures that long life and vigor could best be ensured by saintly behavior.

Even religious figures who do not achieve the reputed immortality of the blessed guru Babaji are often thought by their admirers to be able to thwart the physical decay of their bodies for an extraordinary length of time after death. More than a hundred cases of incorruption, as the phenomenon is known, are recorded in the annals of the Roman Catholic church. One of the most bizarre is that of Saint Cecilia, a noble Roman martyred in AD 177. Her execution was bungled by an inexperienced headsman, who only partly decapitated her. For three days she lay dying, with her face to the floor and her hands crossed in prayer. Then she was buried in that position.

More than a millennium later, in 1599, the basilica dedicated to Saint Cecilia was restored, and her original cypress coffin was discovered there inside a marble sarcophagus. When the coffin lid was pried open, according to reports from the large audience that attended, Saint Cecilia's body was found to be completely intact and still in its dying position—with the neck wound still visible.

Black magic features in many tales as a technique for overcoming the normal limits of mortal life. Many traditional stories tell of characters such as Doctor Faustus, a learned German who pledged his soul to the devil in exchange for youth, knowledge, and magical powers. Such tales may have been inspired by real-life alchemists and magicians in the Middle Ages, trying to make themselves or their paying clients eternally young.

There were clients aplenty eager to pay for the service. Wealth and fame often rewarded those who learned to take advantage of the desire to live forever, and to exploit the public's faith in quack medicines that promised not only to cure illness but to restore the vigor of youth. Itinerant peddlers and respected alchemists alike dispensed widely sold potions that became as well known by their brand names—The Red Dragon, for instance, or The Swan—as patent medicines would be in a later era. Some of the concoctions may have helped cure down-to-earth ills; the discipline of folk medicine, after all, was developed over centuries of trial and error. But when it came to extending life and renewing youth, the claims made for various elixirs were as fantastic as their ingredients, as evidenced by the recipe for this reputed cure-all:

"Pulverize and pass through a sieve an ounce of soccotrine aloes, one drachm of zedoary, one drachm of gentian, one of the finest saffron, one of the finest rhubarb, one of white agaric, one of Venice treacle, one of kina, and place in a bottle, add a pint of good brandy, place whole in shade for nine days, shaking it in the morning and evening. Open on tenth day, add more brandy, filter."

When drunk, according to its creator, this marvelous medication "transforms the body, removes its harmful parts, its incompleteness, and transforms its crudity into a pure, noble and indestructible being." Whatever else the elixir did, its alcohol content undoubtedly provided a "pure,

Flourishing a Latin banner reading "Let us pursue the nature of the shattered elements," an alchemist seeks the elixir of life in this richly ornamented page from a seventeenth-century text.

A happy infant smiles through the infirmities of age in this 1885 advertisement for a patent medicine unappetizingly named Burdock Blood Bitters. Herbs and alcohol were the bases of many such supposedly rejuvenating preparations.

BURDOCK BLOOD BITTERS

BURDOCK Blood BITTERS

AT 3 YEARS OF AGE AND AT 60

COPYRIGHT 1885. OVER

FOSACK & CO. BUFFALO, N.Y.

noble'' vision to some imbibers.

One excellent sales technique of those days was to claim that a panacea had been discovered or invented by one of the more acclaimed alchemists of the time. Medieval Europe supported hundreds of these protoscientists, whose laboratories were filled with experiments aimed at transmuting base metals into gold and discovering formulas for eternal youth. Alchemy was probably introduced to Europe by the Arabs, who were particularly active in the arcane arts in the seventh century AD. Like all their followers, they sought to find and isolate the universal agent, often called the philosophers' stone, with which all things—gold, youth, life itself—could be fashioned. One Arab name for this magical substance was *al iksir,* a term that survives in English as *elixir.*

The alchemic search for the elixir that promised eternal youth gained force in Europe during the twelfth century, spreading with the return of Crusaders from the Middle East. Roger Bacon, one of the most learned men of the thirteenth century, thought humankind had lost the longevity that characterized life before the Flood by immoral behavior and poor personal hygiene. He recommended clean living and, as for himself, became a Franciscan monk.

But he also believed that alchemy could prolong the contemporary life span—then about 50 years—to more than 130 years. Bacon cited numerous cases of "secret arts" that lengthened life. A typical story was that of a man who uncovered a golden jar while plowing a Sicilian field. In the jar was a wondrous liquid; when the plowman drank it and used some to wash his face, he was "renewed in mind and body beyond measure." Bacon never discovered an elixir, but he survived nonetheless to the advanced age of 80.

Of Bacon's successors, perhaps the most famous was a Swiss-born physician and alchemist who took the name

A wrinkled and bloated Pope Innocent VIII is said to have attempted to extend his life through a transfusion of the blood of young boys.

Paracelsus (meaning "beyond Celsus," a renowned first-century Roman physician). The son of a mining engineer, Paracelsus learned metallurgy as a boy and got his medical training not only from doctors but from barbers, midwives, sorcerers, and alchemists. He was an early champion of the idea that a disease could have a chemical basis and might thus be treated with chemicals. In laying a foundation for the more scientific approach to medicine that gradually took hold in succeeding generations, Paracelsus made a significant contribution to the quest for a better, longer life.

Yet he, too, hoping to find a quick solution to the enigma of death, touted an elixir of immortality. His recipe called for a mixture of gold and salt to be steeped in horse dung for four months and then purified by a variety of procedures. Administered daily in "a good wine," it would make "all diseases of the body and mind pass away"—not to mention nails, hair, teeth, and skin, which would grow anew after falling out.

Whether Paracelsus risked the side effects of his concoction is unknown. In any event, the mixture was not enough to protect the alchemist's own life against the hazards of his habits and behavior: He died at forty-eight in a barroom brawl in Salzburg.

The use of alchemy in the search for long life was not confined to Western cultures. The Orient has a long tradition of preparing life-extending potions as well. Ancient Hindu medicine, known as Ayurveda, had a branch called Kaya Kulp, the science of rejuvenation. Within that realm, a major area of inquiry was *rasayana,* the study of potions, whose most popular product was called soma, an organic elixir alleged to rejuvenate the whole body. According to one text, the preparation of soma was as important as its

ingredients and was an intricate business known only to adepts. The elixir called for climbing asparagus, yam, ginkgo fruit, wild dill, wild fennel, and at least one component whose identity was secret. However, according to a different Hindu medical text, the *Sushruta Samhita,* soma is not a mixture of ingredients but the juice of a single plant created by the gods to forestall decay and death; it is reportedly visible only to the most pious and grateful believers.

The text goes on to describe an elaborate ritual wherein the potion does its magic work. The patient enters an inner chamber after scouring his system with emetics and purgatives. Seven harrowing days follow. After drinking carefully administered potions of soma, the patient vomits blood, breaks out in swellings, and ''worms creep out from all parts of the body." The muscles wither and fingernails and hair fall out. During this period the body expels "all filth and obnoxious matter accumulated in the organism through errors in diet and conduct." On the eighth day, rejuvenation begins. Muscles, fingernails, and hair grow again, and "the skin will assume the soft hue of a blue lotus or of a ruby stone." The beautiful figure who finally emerges will "witness ten thousand summers on earth in the full enjoyment of a new and youthful body."

Yet another Hindu recipe for longevity was so-called viper waters, a potion that was credited with according the members of some tribes a life span of 400 years. The brew was prepared annually in spring and served to users in the morning, on an empty stomach, for fifteen days. (Snakes were thought by many societies to offer promise of rejuvenation. It was common belief in medieval Europe, for instance, that when snakes shed their skins they renewed themselves; not unreasonably, alchemists and physicians thought that snake flesh would work the same miracle on humans. French author Harcouët de Langeville discussed a cure for age in which patients would eat nothing but the flesh of chickens that had been fed minced vipers.)

Elsewhere in the East, Taoism, the ancient Chinese religious tradition that reached its pinnacle about 300 BC, also employed alchemy. The fundamental element of Taoism was the concept of the Tao—the ineffable true reality that is the source of all things. Proper living could lead to union with the Tao, a happy state that included, among other benefits, eternal life. Taoist lore was also replete with tales of *xian,* humans who practiced yoga and alchemy to achieve immortality. Over the centuries, many Taoists began to concentrate more on controlling nature in this fashion than in seeking harmony with it.

Taoist alchemical techniques for gaining immortality relied heavily on gold and on cinnabar, a mercury ore that is also a deadly poison. Hopeful oldsters paid well for these longevity potions, even though some were demonstrably fatal. Historians suspect that during the Tang Dynasty, which reigned from AD 618 to 907, seven rulers who tried a

variety of these rejuvenating elixirs died from the effects.

A happier fate is ascribed to Wei Poyang, an important alchemist and author of the oldest known treatise dealing with elixirs of immortality. Wei went into the mountains with three disciples to make his own elixir. When it was completed, Wei fed it first to a dog, which promptly fell down dead. Turning to his disciples, Wei asked whether he should take the elixir, then answered his own question. Having abandoned the world, leaving behind family and friends to seek the Tao of the immortals, he could not turn back. Dying of the elixir, he concluded, could be no worse than living without the Tao.

ei lifted the potion to his lips and slumped lifeless to the ground. One of his students decided to follow his master's example; he too fell dead. The remaining two disciples, lacking their brother's faith, decided that everyday life, even with its pain and sorrow, was preferable to a supposed immortality accessible only by instant death. They abandoned the bodies of the men and dog and descended to a nearby town. After they had left, however, Wei, his loyal follower, and the dog were all restored to life. Before leaving to join the immortals, Wei wrote a letter to the doubting disciples, pointing out that they had let their chance at immortality slip away. When the two found the letter but not their master, the story concludes wistfully, they were "filled with sadness and regret."

The search for life-prolonging energy was never confined entirely to chemical and organic potions. Human sexual energy was understandably viewed as a potent force for rejuvenation, and a variety of sexual themes recur in traditional attempts to achieve immortality. Not surprisingly, in societies unequivocally dominated by men, virtually all the recorded schemes for transmuting the sex drive into a force for extending life were devised from the male point of view.

In the Old Testament, for example, the aging King David was advised to ward off the ailments of his advanced

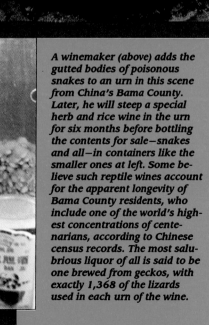

A winemaker (above) adds the gutted bodies of poisonous snakes to an urn in this scene from China's Bama County. Later, he will steep a special herb and rice wine in the urn for six months before bottling the contents for sale—snakes and all—in containers like the smaller ones at left. Some believe such reptile wines account for the apparent longevity of Bama County residents, who include one of the world's highest concentrations of centenarians, according to Chinese census records. The most salubrious liquor of all is said to be one brewed from geckos, with exactly 1,368 of the lizards used in each urn of the wine.

A Banquet Held Once Every 3,000 Years

In Taoist lore, immortality is the reward of those who lead solitary lives of ascetic virtue, acquiring so much vital force that they continue to exist after their bodies die. Having shed their physical shells like cocoons, such immortals travel through the universe, enjoying perfect happiness. They meet at peach banquets given by Xi Wang Mu, Queen Mother of the West.

Long ago, Xi Wang Mu joined with the male god Mu Kung to engender heaven, earth, and all living beings.

Now she lives in the Kunlun mountains (below), guarding a magical tree that bears peaches capable of conferring immortality. The fruit ripens on her birthday every 3,000 years.

The celestial feast that follows (opposite, above) includes not only fresh peaches, but also such exotic fare as monkey lips, bear paws, dragon livers, and phoenix marrow. According to one ancient text, the meal is "festive," with "music on invisible instruments, and songs not from mortal tongues."

In an eighteenth-century soapstone carving, the Taoist longevity god Shou-lao holds a peach containing a miniature crane. The fruit and the bird are common Chinese symbols of long life.

The Kunlun mountains, here glowing through a mist, are said to house Xi Wang Mu's nine-tiered city of gold next to the elusive Lake of Gems.

Symbols of eternal rebirth, a pair of phoenixes spread iridescent wings in the eighteenth-century embroidered silk below. Marrow from the mythical birds' bones is said to be a delicacy of the peach banquets.

In the eighteenth-century Chinese tapestry above, Xi Wang Mu arrives seated on a phoenix (upper left corner) as one of her peach banquets begins. On the platform she is approaching, the gods of happiness, wealth, and longevity greet Xi Wang Mu's other immortal guests.

years by seeking the company of a young virgin. The king's servants scoured Israel for a suitable candidate and returned with a beautiful maiden named Abishag. She nursed King David, waited on him, and lay with him to provide warmth, although the two never "knew" each other in the biblical sense. The king's response to Abishag's ministrations is not recorded, but the treatment seems only to have made his last days more pleasant, not longer.

A citizen of ancient Rome appeared to have better luck with the same concept, which today is known as the practice of gerocomy. According to one report, a man named L. Clodius Hermippus is reputed to have lived 115 years; the epitaph on his tombstone, supposedly found centuries later, credited his longevity to "the aid of the breath of young women, much to the amazement of his physicians." The inscription ended with a recommendation to "lead your life accordingly."

The chronicler of Hermippus's method was a physician, Cohausen by name, who in the eighteenth century wrote a treatise that laid down guidelines "for Prolonging the Life and Vigor of Man." Cohausen's theory was that with every exhalation, people breathe out some "particles" of their essential selves. Those particles could transmit their qualities to anyone who breathed them in, spreading good and bad effects alike. Thus, Cohausen reasoned, an old man surrounded for several hours by healthy young people would breathe their exhalations, imbuing himself with the very essence of youth. Among the other cases Cohausen cited was that of a Venetian who died at 115, having had "five wives and fifteen or twenty concubines, all of them young and beautiful women." Whether the venerable Venetian really lived 115 years is debatable; whether his wives and concubines aged more quickly for having breathed the exhalations of the old man was not recorded.

For those whose resources were more limited, Cohausen revealed another technique for distilling the beneficial particles from human breath. Five young virgins were to be confined to beds in a small room, in the spring of the year. The air in the room would seep through a hole in the

To obtain the extended life offered by this twelfth-century Taoist paper talisman, its owner was meant to burn it and swallow its ashes with water.

wall into a bottle exposed to the cool outside air. The vapors from the virginal exhalations would condense in the bottle, providing an elixir of life. "A few drops of it," wrote Cohausen, "given in the beginning of an acute distemper, resolves and disperses the morbidic matter."

The thirteenth-century English scholar Roger Bacon also recommended the rejuvenating breath of a virgin to ward off old age. As a devout Franciscan monk, however, he was careful to admonish against licentious behavior.

Such circumspection was distinctly absent from the Taoist approach to immortality. Taoists considered sexual abstinence unhealthy, and like some other Eastern philosophies, such as Tantrism, Taoism extolled ritualized sexual practices as a key to long life. For the Taoists, the key to immortality was the preservation of ching, a potent fluid identified with male semen and female menstrual fluid. In order to both preserve the ching and still experience intercourse, a male Taoist adept was enjoined to practice coitus reservatus, always stopping short of his own orgasm while bringing his partner to a climax. The semen thus held in check was thought to invigorate and rejuvenate the man's entire system.

To obtain the maximum advantage, according to Taoist thought, the adept should engage in this activity a dozen or more times in a single day and night, preferably with a number of different partners. Finally, the women should be between fourteen and nineteen years old; older women were supposed to be deficient in the ching needed to build up the adept's immortality account.

While modern researchers tend to agree that sexual activity in moderation is beneficial to health, some findings are confusing. The Shakers, a Utopian society that thrived in nineteenth-century America, abjured sexual contact entirely. At the turn of the century, the Shakers' life expectancy was sixty-seven years—while that of the rest of the population was merely forty-seven. The comparison may be skewed, however, by a function of self-selection: The Shakers were adults when they joined the society and had therefore already survived childhood, whereas a high infant mortality rate necessarily lowered the average life expectancy in the general population.

Even arcane sexual and alchemic recipes for a long life cannot banish the awareness of death's inevitability. And so savants and dreamers through the ages have looked to far-distant or even imaginary lands for a promise that extended life might be attainable after all. The philosophers of ancient Greece wrote longingly of the Hyperboreans—literally, those who live "beyond the north wind." These fortunate beings enjoyed a thousand years of youth in a land of perpetual sunshine. When finally satiated with life, the Hyperboreans brought about their own ends by leaping into the sea.

Legends from Hindu, Persian, Celtic, and Chinese peoples have included accounts of similar outposts of immortality, all of them virtually inaccessible. A modern counterpart is the mountain-locked valley of Shangri-la, described in James Hilton's 1933 novel *Lost Horizon.* Hilton's fictional happy valley of extraordinary longevity was discovered by survivors of a downed airplane that crashed far off course in an impregnable fastness of the Himalayas.

Perhaps it is not surprising, then, that contemporary scientists as well have journeyed to remote corners of the world in search of long-lived peoples and their secrets. In the 1970s, a trio of localities drew the attention of experts: the Caucasus Mountains of the Soviet Union, the Hunza Valley of northern Pakistan, and the Andean village of Vilcabamba in Ecuador.

Certain similarities among the three were immediately apparent. All are mountainous regions, and all are far from the urban areas where an increasing proportion of the

Chosen to warm and revitalize the aged King David by her presence, the young Shunammite maiden Abishag arrives at the royal bedside in this nineteenth-century engraving. According to the Bible, the treatment failed; David died not long after at the age of seventy.

world's population now lives. All seemed to possess considerably more than their share of centenarians, most of whom enjoyed excellent health and continued to be productive members of society. For example, statistics available in the 1970s showed that the proportion of centenarians in different areas of the Caucasus ranged from 39 to 103 per 100,000 inhabitants. At the time, the comparable figure for the United States was 3 per 100,000.

According to American anthropologist Sula Benet, who spent several years studying the Caucasian people, they have been known for their longevity since ancient times. Greek, Persian, and Arabian chronicles mention the long-lived peoples in the mountains between the Black and Caspian seas. Since the 1930s, Soviet gerontologists have been studying the old people of the Caucasus, trying to determine not only how old they are—a difficult task in areas where literacy is rare and written records virtually nonexistent—but also how they maintain a health and vigor that is in stark contrast to the debility common even at younger ages in other societies.

One Soviet gerontologist counted 15,000 citizens of the republic of Georgia who were over the age of eighty. Almost two-thirds of the group took care of themselves without help; only 7 percent were altogether dependent on others. One-quarter of the oldsters regularly walked from one village to another, and an additional 45 percent enjoyed daily strolls around their gardens. A number who were past the age of ninety still worked at their lifelong jobs.

Visiting researchers and journalists found a rich trove of anecdotes about the energetic elderly of the Caucasus. Temur Tarba, a 100-year-old native of Abkhazia, delighted in demonstrating his skillful horsemanship. His friend Markhti Tarkil, 104, daily clambered down a difficult slope to bathe in the frigid waters of a mountain river. At an alleged 117, Gabriel Chapnian routinely worked half days in the fields, going up and down hills that exhausted much younger Western researchers.

The one who gained the most notoriety, though, was tiny, white-haired Khfaf Lasuria, acclaimed as the world's oldest living woman. When she died in 1975, her age was variously given as somewhere between 128 and 141. The celebration of her professed 140th birthday in 1974 was a national Soviet occasion that drew television crews and a delegation from Moscow.

In 1972, Lasuria was interviewed by American physician Alexander Leaf, who decided at the time that she was at least 131. Only two years earlier, she had stopped working on the local collective farm where, in the 1940s and already claiming to be over 100 years old, she had been the farm's fastest tea-leaf picker. A typical day for Lasuria began with a small glass of vodka; lunch included a glass of wine, and by day's end she would have smoked a pack of cigarettes. She was still vigorous in her retirement, playing with great-grandchildren, tending a large vegetable garden, sweeping a large courtyard every day, and completely taking care of her own needs, including laundry. To visit relatives in a distant village, the dauntless great-grandmother simply boarded a bus and rode off alone.

ews of Lasuria's great age drew widespread publicity but was not universally believed, at least in part because of discrepancies in the various accounts she gave of her life story. For example, in talking with Alexander Leaf, she shared a memory of the time in her youth when her first husband considered, but decided against, leaving home to fight in a "big war in the north"—the Crimean War of 1853. Two years later, when interviewed by Russian-speaking Sula Benet, Lasuria told of fleeing her homeland on a Turkish boat during the Crimean War when she was a young girl. In this version of the story, she didn't return for ten years and was first married only at the age of forty.

Anthropologists suggest that such confusions are not surprising. Where few can read or write, storytelling is not only a form of amusement but also the primary means of preserving a tribe's history. Decades of tales told by relatives and neighbors in small villages pass along a wealth of detailed knowledge about the major and minor events that

In these still photos, the motions of Chinese citizens practicing the ancient art of t'ai chi ch'uan (above) seem similar to the movements of aerobics enthusiasts (right) working up a sweat in Denver, Colorado. But the two exercise groups are pursuing longevity in nearly opposite ways. Aerobics practitioners rely on repetitive, vigorous calisthenics to strengthen the heart and lungs, while t'ai chi adepts employ flowing, contemplative poses to enhance suppleness, to cultivate a balance of two inner forces called yin and yang, and to achieve serenity and detachment.

shaped the lives of their ancestors. Any mind crammed with a century's worth of such memories is bound to get confused once in a while. Furthermore, in societies that accord great respect to their oldest members, it is only natural that some of the elderly might slip ancestral stories into their personal histories to bolster their own claims to extraordinary age. But even allowing for the unintentional confusions of memory, Khfaf Lasuria's muddled accounts added to the doubts about her alleged 140 years.

Similar doubts were raised by the longevity claims of centenarians living in distant Hunza, in northern Pakistan (pages 47-55). According to their own testimony, the lives of the Hunzakuts, as they are called, often stretch to a century or more. There is reason to believe that such testimony has itself sometimes stretched the bonds of truth, but there is no doubting the hardiness and good health of the elderly Hunzakuts. Robert McCarrison, a British army surgeon stationed in India during the early twentieth century, noted the general fitness of the population and reported that their wounds and infections healed with remarkable rapidity. McCarrison, an authority on nutrition and public health, credited this well-being to the sparse Hunza diet, largely composed of grains and vegetables. In experiments later in his career, McCarrison found that laboratory rats raised on a Hunzakut diet lived longer and were healthier than rats fed the foods of other cultures.

On the other side of the world from Hunza, the town of Vilcabamba ("sacred valley" in the language of the Inca) lies nestled nearly a mile high between peaks of the Andes in southern Ecuador. Like residents of Soviet Georgia and the Hunza Valley, Vilcabamba's citizens, too, seem to enjoy particularly long lives. A 1971 census numbered its population at 819, including 9 people over the age of 100—a rate hundreds of times higher than in the United States, and more than seventeen times higher than in the Caucasus.

Visitors to Vilcabamba in the 1970s found that the town's elders had much in common with the Caucasians and the Hunzakuts. Many were still lively participants in the life of the town, working in fields, shops, and homes and socializing with their neighbors. Most lived on a subsistence diet of grains and vegetables, with little meat or fat of any kind. All enjoyed great respect within their families and the community. But here, too, researchers had problems judging the real ages of the oldest inhabitants.

Alexander Leaf—who studied the longevous peoples of Hunza and Vilcabamba as well as of the Caucasus at first hand—cites the case of Miguel Carpio as an example. In 1970 Carpio claimed to be 121 years old. Since most of the town's residents were Roman Catholics, baptismal records provided a means for verifying some claimed ages, but there was no record of Carpio's birth. Baptismal records for his siblings, however, indicated that Carpio was probably no more than 106 years old—still a venerable age. The gentleman himself complicated the issue further, when Leaf returned four years later and found Carpio's claimed age had increased by eleven years, to 132. More detailed research by later investigators using church records and family interviews seemed to show that the typical so-called centenarian of Vilcabamba was probably about 85 years old.

Soviet gerontologist Zhores Medvedev had similar experiences in the Caucasus, but in these cases, he suggested, some of the discrepancies may have arisen when young men adopted the identities of dead ancestors to avoid conscription into the army. Alexander Leaf subsequently reexamined the plausibility of the age claims he had accepted in his first round of studies of centenarians. "We now know those ages in Ecuador and the Caucasus are rubbish," Leaf admitted. He said he and other researchers had been misled, in part by Ecuadoran or Georgian doctors who relayed the age claims without checking them first.

Not everyone agrees with such hard-nosed scientific certainty. In a 1976 book about her Caucasian studies entitled How to Live to be 100, Sula Benet argues that denial of the old-age claims of her subjects is based on ignorance and envy. "It often seems to me," she writes, "that the doubters actually do not want to believe that people live to

such great ages anywhere in the world, especially in the Soviet Union." Anthropologist Benet rejects the gerontologists' idea of a maximum life span. Just because no one with a documented birth date has ever survived beyond the age of 115, she says, does not mean it is impossible. Such limits, she argues spiritedly, "set psychological limits, reinforce hopelessness among the old, and contribute nothing to our understanding."

Support for Benet's perspective comes from psychologist Robert Morgan in his 1982 book *Growing Younger*. For one thing, Morgan suggests that living in the mountains, specifically at heights of between 5,000 and 10,000 feet, may well have a salubrious effect on aging persons. "Among people living at high altitudes," he writes, "there is a higher oxygen-carrying capacity per unit volume of blood and a generally expanded blood volume. The lungs must work harder to carry the oxygen and the body must exert itself more in normal activity."

Morgan urges the application of such scientific knowledge to help eradicate the debilitating afflictions that accompany old age, but he rejects the argument that the human body has a specific shelf life of, say, 115 years. "If we were to use everything science has taught us to date," he writes optimistically, "I feel that 140 years would be a reasonable expectation for the human life span—a vigorous, youthful 140 years at that. Spectacular breakthroughs in genetics and organ regeneration would take us even farther."

Whatever the truth of the claims for extreme age—and most researchers today doubt claims greater than 115 years—scientists acknowledge that many of the old people they have studied in the world's remote bastions of longevity are remarkably healthy. Their way of life tends to confirm what most Western doctors, nutritionists, gerontologists, and exercise enthusiasts already preach: regular and vigorous physical activity, a diet low in fat and high in complex carbohydrates, moderation in the consumption of alcohol, and a generally low level of mental and emotional stress. The most notable item the example of these remote long-lived peoples would add to that list is, perhaps, not surprising either: no retirement. They continue to be active, useful members of society until they literally can work no longer, reaping all the emotional benefits that attend being productive and needed.

Roy Walford, the gerontologist who noted that the desire for physical immortality is "humanity's oldest dream," says he has extended the maximum life span of fish in his UCLA laboratory by up to 300 percent. He urges that steps be taken now to start pushing back "the outer limit" of human longevity. "It's high time," wrote Walford. "Not only for fish, but for us."

Others share or exceed his confidence in the possibilities. Arthur C. Clarke, the visionary writer of science and science fiction whose perceptiveness and lucid prose have made him a leading authority on the future, has pronounced immortality to be not only possible but probably unavoidable. Death, he writes "does not appear to be biologically inevitable. . . . Because biological immortality and the preservation of youth are such potent lures, men will never cease to search for them. . . . It would be foolish to imagine that this search will never be successful, down all the ages that lie ahead."

But, warns Clarke, "whether success would be desirable is quite another matter." Another author, Osborn Segerberg, Jr., expands on that issue. "The promise, the

commitment of biological gerontology," he has written, "is to make the phrase 'and they lived happily ever after' come true. However, molecular biologists cannot be expected to guarantee the happiness part." Indeed, asks Segerberg, would all humans be happy if they lived forever? Or would they be bored?

Moreover, the practical, ethical, and spiritual questions arising from a world that has banished natural death would be legion. If there were no growing old, no need for retirement, no "ages of man," could society modify its patterns of family structure and economic growth? What would become of parents and children over such long spans of time? Would all members of society or only a privileged few have access to life-prolonging techniques? How could the globe support the population explosion that would follow? What would become of religious commitment—what would happen to God—if there were no death?

The questions are perhaps unanswerable at this stage; but they raise troubling doubts. One man who had a strong opinion on the subject was the author Joseph Conrad. In 1921, long before most of the questions had even been raised in any serious context, he wrote emphatically: "What humanity needs is not the promise of scientific immortality, but compassionate pity in this life and infinite mercy on the Day of Judgement."

Yet, as Clarke points out, the lure of a longer life is too strong for humankind to resist. Technology is poised on the brink of a critical advance toward making the age-old dream come true, and for most people, scientists or laypeople, it is an exhilarating prospect.

Roy Walford expressed that excitement when he explained why he chose at an early age to dedicate himself to a search for the extension of life: "It seemed to me (and still does) that a person's allotted span of life is simply too short to permit a satisfying exploration of the world's outer wonders and the realms of inner experience. We are cut off in the midst of our pleasures, separated too soon from our loved ones, shelved at the mere beginning of our understanding, and laughed at by the gods."

The Real Shangri-la

In his novel *Lost Horizon,* James Hilton described a hidden Himalayan valley called Shangri-la, where people aged so slowly that a centuries-old woman was smooth-skinned and beautiful, and equally ancient men were as vigorous as youths. The place was imaginary, but an actual valley in the mountains of northern Pakistan shares so many of the fictional land's characteristics—including unusually fit and long-lived old people—that it has been described as a real-life Shangri-la.

The valley is called Hunza, and its people Hunzakuts. Dazzled by the health of aged Hunzakuts, travelers have extolled everything from the valley's simple lifestyle to its mineral-laden waters as the secret of long life. Health researchers see some metaphorical snakes in this seeming paradise, including a high infant-mortality rate and disease-bearing parasites in the fabled waters. Nonetheless, many inhabitants undeniably do continue productive work through their eighties and nineties.

Their own explanations include rigorous physical labor and a diet of fruit, vegetables, and grains. "To live long," said an old Hunza farmer, "work hard and eat traditional things." Another factor is the effective natural selection imposed by infant diseases. One Hunzakut put it bluntly: "Those of us who live are strong. Those who are not strong die." Others credit happy families and low stress levels. "I have just one piece of advice for young people who wish to live long," a Hunzakut said. "The first thing is happiness. If anything makes you happy, you should use it."

A flourishing oasis nestled in the midst of the snow-capped peaks of Pakistan's Karakoram Mountains, the Hunza Valley is accessible even today by only a single road. Of the inhabitants' extreme isolation, a British researcher observed in 1938: "They have preserved their remoteness from the ways and habits of the modern world and with it those methods of life which contribute or cause the excellent physique and bodily health which is theirs."

Bearded like a biblical patriarch, a smiling Hunza elder hoists a load to his shoulder with the agility of a youth. Respected for their wisdom, the oldest Hunzakuts have traditionally helped govern the tiny state, meeting each morning to arbitrate disputes and establish rules. "By being continually challenged in this manner by younger colleagues they retained their mental faculties," wrote physician Alexander Leaf, who visited the Hunza in 1971.

At threshing time in a Hunza wheat field (opposite), a boy stands next to a team of oxen that is driven over the cut stalks to separate the grain from the straw. Accustomed to hard labor from an early age, young children are often assigned to follow work animals with a basket or pan in hand to catch and save the precious, fertilizing manure as it falls.

Workers climbing the hillside below carry rocks and soil to maintain the masonry-walled terraces on which their crops grow (left). Tending the plots of grains, beans, and vegetables requires constant clambering up and down steep slopes, which may add years to Hunza-kuts' lives by promoting cardio-vascular health and fending off bone-weakening osteoporosis.

Called "glacial milk" because of its pearly gray color, water melted from distant glaciers cascades down a rocky stream (right). Modern spectrum analysis has shown that this murky-looking, silt-laden water—which the Hunzakuts drink in vast quantities and use to irrigate their fields—contains most of the trace minerals that are essential for optimal health.

A Hunza woman milks a goat while her child watches over the herd. Milk, preserved as cheese, buttermilk, or a soured form akin to yogurt, is one of the few high-fat elements in the Hunzakut diet, which on average contains about two-thirds the calories and only one-third the fat consumed by a typical American. Current research on rodents suggests that caloric restriction—or undernutrition, as it is called—can extend life.

Above, apricots are spread on a rocky ledge to dry for use in the autumn and winter months. Rich in health-promoting trace minerals, apricots along with other fruits are a staple of the high-fiber, low-fat Hunza diet, which includes a high proportion of vegetables and whole grains—foods that are recognized for their role in prolonging life by guarding against cancer and heart disease.

Typifying the affectionate nature of Hunza family life, a mother cuddles her infant while an adolescent girl stands close by. Mothers lay a sturdy foundation for their children's health by breast-feeding them well into toddlerhood—a practice that provides excellent nutrition and guards against early childhood disease. Traditionally, girls are nursed to the age of two; boys are breast-fed until they are three years old.

A young man dances in a festival called a buzzum, described by one Hunzakut as "a party with music, dancing, wine and gin—everything except girls." Some Hunzakuts claim that buzzums help them live longer, a view supported by studies indicating that moderate drinkers tend to outlive teetotalers.

Mallet-swinging horsemen gallop full tilt down one of the narrow polo fields that take up the few precious yards of level ground in many villages. Polo, a sport that requires lightning reflexes and makes rigorous physical demands, is a staple of Hunza life, played from childhood until well into old age.

CHAPTER 2

Seeking an Answer in Science

Trumpeted the review that appeared in the *Chicago Sun-Times,* "If it's true, it's the greatest scientific breakthrough since nuclear fission. The repercussions are enormous." The book that so impressed the reviewer, titled *In His Image: The Cloning of a Man,* was published as nonfiction in 1978, and the chilling story contained in its pages set the scientific community—and, indeed, anyone who read it—abuzz. It told the story of an elderly millionaire, identified only as Max, who had asked the book's author, David M. Rorvik, to help him in his quest to produce a clone of himself.

A clone is an organism grown from the cells of one parent, instead of being produced by sexual means from the cells of two parents. Because a clone receives all its genes from a single parent, those genes are exactly the same as the parent's genes and direct the organism to develop in precisely the same form as the parent. According to Rorvik, Max had read some of the author's previous books and articles on genetics and cloning, and he wanted Rorvik to help him find a physician to perform the cloning procedure. Max wanted someone to create a genetic replica of himself, a child who would grow to be, physically at least, another Max, thus giving the old man a kind of continued life or—if the clone later produced another clone, followed by yet more generations of exact reproductions of Max—even a kind of immortality, albeit without continuity of consciousness. The old man also wondered whether he and his clone might not share a mystical rapport, a telepathic link that could somehow, even after death, tether him inextricably to the living world.

Intrigued by the prospect of observing the work firsthand, Rorvik located a gynecologist, whom he called Darwin in the book, and the two men supposedly accompanied Max to an unidentified spot in the tropics, where the millionaire owned rubber plantations, nutmeg trees, and rice paddies. At a hospital that Max had built for his workers, a number of women volunteered to donate the ova needed for the cloning attempt. The donor's own genetic code, contained in an egg's nucleus, would be removed. Then the nucleus of one of Max's body cells would be implanted in the egg, from which a fetus would develop. (According to the author, Darwin refused to disclose which body cells were being used, claiming it would be unfair to the cloned child to be referred to in the future as "one who started life as a piece of bone marrow, a blood cell, or a scrap of cancer.") The egg donor would then serve as a surrogate mother, carrying the fetus to term in her womb. And so, the story continues, in that exotic locale, a child bearing the genetic makeup of its father alone was born in December 1976.

The release of the book, which was an immediate bestseller, created an uproar in the scientific establishment, and soon Rorvik and his publisher were squaring off against genetic experts who claimed that the story was a complete fiction, that the book was filled with errors, and that the author had misrepresented the work of distinguished scientists. Within a few months of publication, Oxford University geneticist J. Derek Bromhall filed suit against Rorvik and his publisher, J. B. Lippincott, claiming that the author had used his name in the book without permission and that a portion of the cloning technique described by Rorvik was based on one that Bromhall had developed for use on rabbits.

The case eventually went to court, and in a preliminary finding the judge ruled the story of Max and his genetic double a "fraud and a hoax," declaring that "the cloning described in the book never took place," and that "all the characters mentioned in the book, other than the defendant Rorvik, have no real existence." Although Rorvik remained steadfast in his claims that Max and the child

did indeed exist, publisher Lippincott settled the case out of court with Bromhall for a reported $100,000, sent him a letter of apology, and openly stated that they now believed the book to be fiction. But the book's release and the ensuing public debate served to focus attention on a little-known field of research that could have an astonishing impact on the future of humankind.

Suddenly people who had never before heard the word *clone*—from the Greek for "twig"—were reading news accounts describing various cloning procedures. Experts explained methods that had been used to clone such animals as frogs and sheep. They offered their opinions on the possibility of growing—in a laboratory, from a single cell—human organs that would be identical to those inside a person's body. These organs would be transplanted into the cell donor, they explained, replacing those damaged by age, disease, or trauma and restoring the physical functioning of youth. Others knowledgeable in the field of genetics speculated on how an entire human body could be cloned, in ways not unlike those laid out by Rorvik. The duplicate physical form could be frozen, they theorized, until such time as its organs were needed as replacement parts: The clone would perform, in effect, as a personal organ bank, rendering the current notions of aging and maximum life span obsolete.

Understandably, a multitude of questions arose from these discussions. Exactly how close are scientists to finding a way to produce genetically perfect copies of individual human beings? Is the day dawning when humans can choose between dying, living forever through the cloning of organs, or, like the old mil-

Full of imposing dignity in this 1880s photograph, French physiologist Charles-Édouard Brown-Séquard lost face when the rejuvenation therapy he devised proved useless. He has gained posthumous recognition, however, as a pioneer of the field of endocrinology.

lionaire Max in Rorvik's book, seeing, through the eyes of a clone, how life could have been lived if different choices had been made? And what would the clone be like? Its appearance would be identical to the cell donor's, but would it share the same thoughts, desires, likes, and dislikes? And what are the moral implications of such a procedure?

As in the case of most ethical dilemmas, persuasive arguments can be made on all sides of the cloning issue, and it will likely be a hotly debated topic for decades to come. Most experts agree that extending human life through cloning is years of painstaking research away—and then only if the United States government approves such research, which seems unlikely. So while it is an exciting, if controversial, prospect, cloning is but one of many avenues being explored by scientists seeking first to understand the process of aging, then to ultimately defeat or defer death.

At this stage in the research, says gerontologist Richard Weindruch, formerly of the National Institute on Aging in Bethesda, Maryland, and now at the University of Wisconsin, "there are as many theories of aging as there are gerontologists." Nor is there agreement on the prospects for a significant increase in the maximum human life span, considered to be 110 to 120 years. A sizable contingent of investigators in the field believe that even if the underlying mechanisms of aging are identified, science may not be able to alter the biological schedule. It could be that the interplay of contributing factors is so intricate and subtle that no hormone, diet, or drug therapy can ever significantly forestall death.

Simply fending off disease is

not the answer: Although in the industrialized world advances in healthcare during the twentieth century have nearly doubled life expectancy—raising it from about 40 years to more than 70 years—that sort of health-related progress is statistically unsustainable. An assessment of the upper limit of human life expectancy was conducted by researchers at the University of Chicago and at the Argonne National Laboratory in Argonne, Illinois, the results of which were published in the November 1990 issue of the journal *Science*. The report concluded that "further gains in life expectancy will occur, but these will be modest," pushing no higher than age 85 even if science can completely eliminate cancer and heart disease, which account for almost half of all deaths in the United States. (Recent figures estimate the life expectancy at birth for females to be 78.3 years, and that of males to be 71.4 years. For reasons that scientists have yet to fully understand, females outlive males in almost all forms of animal life.)

Still, the subject of life's limits is fraught with unknowns and thus is rich in possibilities for revolutionary findings. Considering the stakes involved—the dream of escape from a sentence of thinning and wrinkling skin, shrinking muscles, dimming senses, stiffening joints, degenerating organs, waning resistance to diseases—it is understandable that gerontology seethes with debate. Few precincts of science are so stirred by hope and urgency, emotions that also drove early attempts to mute the effects of age and infirmity.

In past centuries, medical efforts to overcome the frailties of the body tended to be more mag-

The reddish purple blooms of the bloodwort plant convinced folk medicine practitioners of its ability—now confirmed by modern science—to check bleeding.

ical than scientific. Healers often treated their patients with medicines that seemed to have some physical kinship with the affliction—a resemblance of color or shape, for example. Thus, in medieval times, the red-leafed or red-rooted wild plants called bloodworts were used to treat ailments thought to stem from the heart or blood. It was the same sort of magical thinking that caused some physicians to hit upon the idea that youthful bodies contained an essence of vitality that might be transferred, via the breath or the blood, to an aging body to conquer any infirmities. While they gained little, those oldsters who contrived to breathe the exhalations of vigorous young men or women did themselves no harm, at least; but those who were treated with transfusions of a youth's blood usually suffered the same dire fate that befell Pope Innocent VIII when he tried it in 1492—that is, severe systemic reactions leading to death.

A few centuries later, a related and somewhat safer—if no more effective—approach was espoused by French physiologist and neurologist Charles-Édouard Brown-Séquard. At age seventy-two, the professor of experimental medicine at the Collège de France was approaching the end of a brilliant and varied career. His vocation had ranged

just hours earlier he had passed the final test: "Today I was able to 'pay a visit' to my young wife."

Brown-Séquard drew a direct connection between male sexuality and anatomical fitness, arguing that, once the hormonal balance was corrected by an infusion of minced gonads, the key to longevity lay in keeping semen re-

from practicing midwifery in New York City to describing the physiology of the human spinal cord and contributing landmark work in the new field of endocrinology. Tall and imposing, he enjoyed a reputation for dramatic presentation—which he fully justified in Paris on June 1, 1889, during a lecture before members of the Société de Biologie.

For the last few years, Brown-Séquard told his rapt audience, he had been testing himself with a dynamometer, an instrument that measures mechanical force. As was perhaps to be expected, the device had revealed the debilitating effects of aging on his muscles. He then described the fatigue and sleeplessness that had rendered him unable to perform as a husband with the young woman he had recently married. But all that had changed, Brown-Séquard declared, as a result of the experiment he had begun just a few weeks earlier.

The assembled scientists—many of whom were even older than the speaker—listened intently as Brown-Séquard described his methodology: He had injected himself with filtered extracts from the crushed testicles of young dogs and guinea pigs. The effects, he told them, were remarkable. Not only did dynamometer tests indicate renewed muscle strength, but Brown-Séquard reported he had also regained the vigor and intellectual stamina of his youth. Once again he could stand in his laboratory for hours on end, work long into the night, and run up staircases. And best of all,

serves carefully calibrated, never letting too much accumulate or drawing stores down too low. A sensation followed. Besieged by aging but eager Frenchmen, Brown-Séquard built a complicated machine that pulped and filtered bull testes to produce a supposedly rejuvenating fluid. A Paris newspaper started a fund for an Institute of Rejuvenation that would promulgate the Méthode Séquardienne.

The scientific community, however, reacted savagely, deriding Brown-Séquard's purported results as senile delusions. A Vienna medical publication called the lecture "further proof of the necessity of retiring professors who have attained their threescore and ten." And the *Boston Medical and Surgical Journal* harshly admonished that "the sooner the general public and especially septuagenarian readers of the latest sensation understand that for the physically used up and worn out there is no secret of rejuvenation, no elixir of youth, the better."

As it turned out, the scientists won the day. No one regained his lost youth and potency from Séquardienne treatments—modern researchers credit Brown-Séquard's own improvement to his positive expectations rather than to any physiological effect—and the professor's reputation never regained its former luster. His career in ruins, Brown-Séquard left Paris. His young wife deserted him, and less than five years after the fateful lecture, he died of a stroke.

The French doctor's demise notwithstanding, his claims of renewed vigor were echoed in the 1890s by a Viennese physiology professor named Eugen Steinach, who sought to reverse the aging process in men by performing vasectomies on them. Some years later, in a best-selling book titled *Rejuvenation through the Experimental Revitalization of the Aging Puberty Gland,* Steinach explained his rationale. The vibrancy of youth, he said, derived from testosterone, whose release was blocked over time by the mechanics of sperm production. Therefore, the recovery of youthfulness was a simple matter. Tying off the vas deferens, the duct that carries sperm from the testicles to the ejaculatory ducts, would permit testosterone to be released once more and youthful vitality restored. The "Steinach rejuvenation operation" luckily brought about no ill after-effects, but neither did it work as advertised. Yet thousands of eager patrons, including such luminaries as the Irish poet William Butler Yeats, sought out the procedure.

As Steinach's popularity swelled, so too did that of Serge Voronoff, a charismatic and cocky Russian-born surgeon. While serving as a physician to the king of Egypt, Voronoff observed that the court eunuchs seemed to age extremely rapidly and that he spent a disproportionate amount of his time treating their illnesses. Like Steinach, he concluded that male hormones played a critical role in maintaining the body's resiliency. Decrepit old men, he declared, are actually eunuchs; they have been emasculated "not by the criminal hand of man but by the cruel law of nature, by the wear and tear of old age." Putting the matter positively, he proclaimed that "possession of active genital glands constitutes that best possible assurance of long life."

Establishing himself in France, Voronoff devised a novel bit of surgery to repair the depredations of age: In 1918 he transplanted the genitals from a two-year-old lamb onto an aging ram whose limbs trembled and whose wool was thin and balding in places. Within three months, according to Voronoff, the ram was transformed—his limbs were steady and his wool thicker, and the animal's sexual vigor had returned. To test his theory further, Voronoff removed the grafted genitals and observed the ram's gradual decline. The surgeon then performed a second transplant, and saw the ram's vitality return. An elated Voronoff declared that "the case of this ram indicates to us the course to be pursued, the ideal to be attained: the prolongation of the length of life and the shortening of the period of old age, thanks to gland-grafting."

Flush with apparent success, Voronoff was now ready to take "gland-grafting" one step further—he planned to use the testicles of strapping, young male volunteers to revitalize elderly men. As one can imagine, few young men were eager to donate such precious parts of their anatomies; those who agreed to give them up demanded top dollar. So the surgeon, taking a glance down the evolutionary ladder, made the logical next choice: He began transplanting bits of chimpanzee and monkey testes onto the genitals of elderly men. More than 1,000 patients underwent the costly "monkey gland treatment," as it was called. Although the vast majority of his patients were men, on at least one occasion Voronoff reportedly grafted the sex glands of a female monkey onto those of a forty-eight-year-old woman, in an effort to "enable this woman to regain her unkind husband by means of charms recovered and graces renewed and freshened." According to his own dubious account, the woman returned two years later looking more than ten years younger and "converted into a charming personality."

Voronoff's worldwide fame and his utter confidence in his work did not change the fact that his treatment was a sham. The lack of drugs to suppress the immune system ensured that a transplant would soon be rejected by the recipient's tissues, and to make matters worse, according to one account, many of the recipients contracted syphilis from the monkey donors. The only benefits of gland-grafting, if any, were owed to the placebo effect, the mind's belief in the efficacy of the treatment.

This message was slow in making it across the Atlantic, however, where Americans, too, were searching for ways to regain their youthful vim and vigor. Many of them were flocking to tiny Milford, Kansas, where, in 1917, a North Carolina drifter named John Romulus Brinkley had set up an office, hung a sheepskin from the Eclectic Medical University of Kansas City—a diploma mill—and begun performing goat-gonad transplants.

Brinkley's first patient was said to be a farmer who complained of being a "flat tire," or impotent. Using one of the farmer's own goats, Brinkley implanted a bit of the animal's gonads in the man's testicles. Just two weeks later the farmer proclaimed the return of his libido, and within a year he had sired a son named, appropriately enough, Billy.

Over the next decade, Brinkley earned a fortune sewing goat testicles into eager patients. Not only did he claim to cure such far-ranging conditions as impotence, insanity, skin diseases, and high blood pressure with his bizarre procedure, but the goat-gland transplant had the alleged added value of "prolonging life and rebuilding the human body." On a good day, 500 people would swarm into the town of Milford seeking rejuvenation at the doctor's hands. Fees started at $750; the price of goats soared.

Brinkley used some of his surgically won wealth to buy three yachts, a fleet of luxury cars, and a radio station from which he pitched his services. In 1930, however, the business that reportedly had made him a millionaire began

John R. Brinkley's bespectacled face suggests a frank, sensitive nature in this 1923 photograph taken with his wife. The Kansas quack's deceptively honest visage may have helped him lure thousands into suffering his oft harmful goat-gland treatment for impotence.

to unravel.

His license to practice medicine was revoked by the state, and he had to hire others to perform the transplants. Finally, in 1941, the doctor retired from practice, prudently shifted most of his holdings to his wife and friends, and declared bankruptcy. Dispiritedly he told the court, "I don't think there is but two Cadillacs left."

While Brinkley and his predecessors insisted that diminished sex hormones alone account for the loss of youthful energy and robustness, another physician of the day, Swiss surgeon and glandular expert Paul Niehans, concluded that the degeneration of the body's cells was a more critical factor in aging. Still, he was no less an optimist than the sex-hormone practitioners. Niehans believed that a reversal of bodily decline might be brought about by replenishing failing cell populations with hordes of dynamic young cells.

Niehans hit upon his treatment—called cellular therapy, or CT—more or less accidentally. In 1931, a woman suffering from a convulsive disorder was referred to him by another physician; her parathyroid glands, responsible for regulating the amount of calcium in the bloodstream, appeared to be diseased. Niehans considered performing a transplant but decided that the patient was too ill to survive the operation. Instead, he tried a long-shot treatment:

He gave her an injection of minced parathyroid of ox, thinking that the cells of the animal might continue to do the calcium-regulating job for a short while in their human host and relieve some of the patient's suffering. The treatment worked far better than Niehans had expected. The woman was soon completely free of her former symptoms—and she stayed that way. "I thought the effect would be short-lived, just like the effect of an injection of hormones," the physician later wrote, "and that I should have to repeat the injection. But to my great surprise the injection of fresh cells not only failed to provoke a reaction but the effect lasted."

Much struck by this outcome, Niehans commenced a series of tests on himself, as well as on other patients and on laboratory animals. His general approach, fine-tuned over decades, involved repeated dosings with minced preparations of organs taken from sheep embryos, which had been removed from the sheep and dissected just minutes before. Sheep were chosen for their resistance to disease and for the rare incidence of allergic reactions in humans

64

when their cells are used therapeutically. Also, Niehans contended that the chemistry of embryonic cells is far more powerful than that of older cells.

The old medieval principle of resemblance led the physician to choose fetal heart cells for heart problems, liver cells for cirrhosis, kidney cells for nephritis, and so on, according to a patient's particular complaint. Like earlier rejuvenation therapists, Niehans greatly valued the therapeutic attributes of the sex glands. These, he said, were a "rich source of vital fluids which give physical strength, intellectual freshness and also physical qualities." In addition, he claimed, they "revitalize the aging organism."

Niehans contended that a single CT treatment resuscitated flagging organs as if they had been entirely replaced, a suggestion that excited many an ailing party in the era predating organ transplantation. Devotees—among them, film actor Charlie Chaplin and statesmen Winston Churchill and Charles de Gaulle—flocked to Clinique La Prairie, Niehans's exclusive establishment on the shores of Lake Geneva. In some cases, Niehans even made house calls: In 1954, he traveled to Italy, where seventy-seven-year-old Pope Pius XII had requested CT treatment for a mysterious gastric ailment. By all accounts the pope's illness abated under the Swiss physician's care, even though Niehans reportedly had to treat the pontiff with freeze-dried cells rather than fresh—live sheep were not allowed in the Vatican.

La Prairie still caters to an international clientele and has spawned numerous imitators: Some two million people have reportedly received CT treatments at clinics in Europe. (Only one clinic, Genesis West, located in Mexico near the California border, currently practices live-cell therapy in North America.) In a typical course of therapy, patients are tested before being treated, supposedly to determine which of their organs lack cells. They are confined to bed for several days after receiving injections and are released from the clinic about a week later. Before leaving La Prairie, patients are advised to protect their precious new cells by avoiding the potentially damaging effects of x-rays, ultraviolet rays, sauna baths, and even very hot hair dryers.

Despite his considerable intellectual attainments, Niehans himself was at a loss to explain how CT actually works. He broadly implied that the vital new cells actually became incorporated into human organs and began pumping out biological factors no longer produced by the worn-out machinery of aged cells. In some respects, CT is reminiscent of therapies employed by healers among the ancient peoples of the Near and Far East, many of whom believed in the rejuvenating effects of the inner organs of wild beasts. An Egyptian papyrus dating from 1500 BC mentions the virtues of ingesting animal viscera. The Hindus once regarded tiger gonads as a cure for impotence, while the Greeks thought that eating the bone marrow of lions endowed a man with courage—advice that Homer's Achilles followed, according to *The Iliad.* Chinese sages went so far as to recommend eating human placentas for a general lift to health.

But modern standards

Black ewes graze at La Prairie's farm, located about thirty-five miles from Montreux in Switzerland. The animals provide a regular harvest of fetuses for use in the clinic's cellular injections (below).

of medicine demand substantial proof before the efficacy of a treatment can be ratified by the scientific establishment, and such proof is lacking for cellular therapy—in the judgment of some authorities, at least. An extensive investigation of the process conducted by the American Medical Association in the 1960s failed to confirm the powers attributed to cellular therapy, but neither did it find CT provably useless. A leading gerontologist has remarked that a trip to La Prairie might be called "Gullibles Travels." Nonetheless, others in the field have hinted off the record that CT may in fact work, though not in the suspected manner. Rather than rejuvenating organs, it may instead stimulate the body's natural defenses. Scientists are only beginning to understand the complex ways in which the disease-fighting powers of the immune system are called into play. Some researchers suggest that CT may serve to energize an immune system on the wane.

Paul Niehans, who died in 1971 at the age of eighty-nine, was sometimes heard to say, "I am no scientist." True enough. But gerontology today falls squarely in the purview of science; it is a methodical investigative activity with strict rules of evidence and a powerful interest in root causes.

Hundreds of researchers are currently attempting to comprehend how the body deteriorates as it grows older and to encapsulate that understanding in a single unified theory of aging, a model of the process that pulls all the disparate facts into a coherent whole. Most of these efforts focus on the cell, which has refused to surrender its deepest secrets after more than a century of near-obsessive scrutiny by biologists. At base, the changes associated with senescence—loss of elasticity in the skin; weakening of bones and muscles; slowed reflexes; and increased susceptibility to disease, especially heart ailments and cancers—are changes that manifest themselves first at the cellular level. While gerontologists generally agree on this central tenet, they diverge in discussing where exactly the wrench is thrown into the cellular machinery. Hypotheses have tended to fall into two broad camps, which might be labeled

the wear-and-tear camp and the biological-clock camp.

Those in the first camp believe aging results from the depredations of life, which gradually disrupt cells at the molecular and even atomic levels. Those in the second camp hold that there is some innate, preprogrammed limit to life, so that at a given point cells simply begin to fail. This failure may be triggered by the genes within the cells, or by hormones released by the pituitary gland, or perhaps by a combination of messages from various bodily systems.

Embraced by these broad categories are a host of theories, each of which has mustered ardent support among researchers. One that has enjoyed much discussion and has spawned several variants is the cellular error theory—the idea that random glitches in cells' DNA, the long chains of nucleic acids that mastermind the chemical workings of an organism, cause the cells to go haywire. DNA serves as a pattern for the production of RNA, a simpler nucleic acid structure, which in turn acts as a template for the synthesis of proteins, the main building blocks of the body. Therefore, any damage to either DNA or RNA translates directly into errors on the protein assembly line. Improperly built proteins, say some researchers, are the culprits in aging.

Humans are constantly exposed to things that can disrupt DNA: gamma, ultraviolet, and x-radiation; drugs; synthetic and naturally occurring chemicals; and even foods. So the error-catastrophe theory of aging, as the notion has come to be called, would seem to make compelling sense. For every individual, damage mounts as time goes by, and so, presumably, do errors in protein manufacture.

But other chemical missteps within cells—errant hookups rather than breakages—complicate the picture. These errors were implicated in the aging process by a young chemist named Johan Bjorksten in 1941. Then working for an American film-manufacturing company, Bjorksten became interested in the way the pliant sheets of gelatin emulsion used in film gradually harden when exposed to air. Gelatin consists of a close-knit mesh of protein

Rhinoceros horns like these in South Africa fetch almost $23,000 a pound on the black market. It has long been believed that East Asians grind them into aphrodisiacs, but some now say the use there is for antifever medicines.

Labeled ginseng roots by smugglers, these dried tiger penises from China (below) were seized by French customs. So many eager buyers believe the organs enhance virility that poachers have pushed the Chinese tiger to the brink of extinction.

Bizarre Jump-Starts for Fading Sex Drives

Because of nature's scheme for survival of the species, the urge and ability to procreate have always been important traits of human youth. Even on today's amply peopled planet, the celebration of youthful sexuality is strong and the loss of desire or potency often feared as a sign of aging.

To counteract the unwelcome sexual changes that sometimes accompany age, people have long sought out aphrodisiacs, remedies made of bizarre ingredients that supposedly bring back satisfying intercourse. The Apache Indians used cow dung in their love potions. The ancient dwellers of India ate the flesh of a white heifer cooked in its mother's milk. And William Shakespeare recommended hot lavender, mints, savory, and marjoram.

Plants or animals that resemble the human phallus are perennially popular in aphrodisiacs. Animal horns, for instance, have long been touted as erotic stimulants. Mandrake and ginseng roots, often shaped like little men, have incurred similar notoriety. Even the rabbit's foot began as a symbol of virility. The foot's phallic shape and the rabbit's reputation for zestful and frequent coupling secured the appendage popularity as a love charm.

Today, folk wisdom credits such substances as shellfish, alcohol, and cantharides—or Spanish fly, a powder made from beetles—with the power to enhance sexuality. But none of these has been proved to incite or improve lovemaking. Alcohol actually impedes it, and cantharides—though it may cause erection—irritates the urinary tract, making intercourse painful.

However, researchers are testing a new drug, quinerolane, which may unlock the secret of lifelong carnal desire. The drug stimulates dopamine, a chemical messenger in the brain that, when active, may boost sex drive.

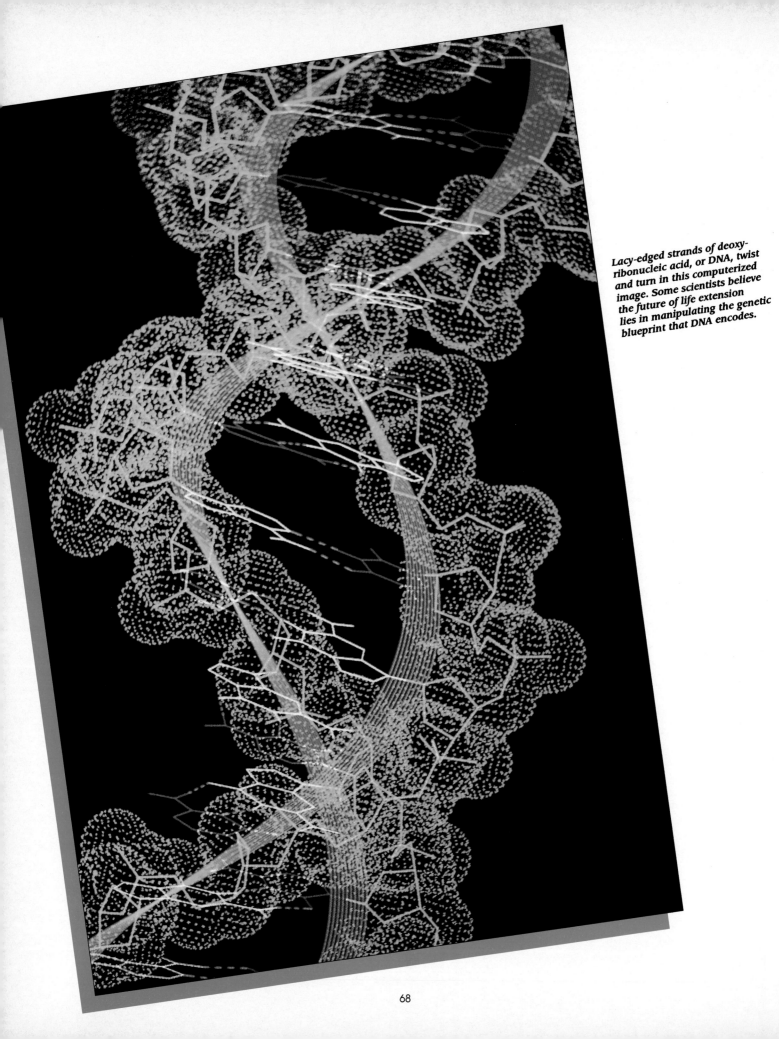

Lacy-edged strands of deoxy-ribonucleic acid, or DNA, twist and turn in this computerized image. Some scientists believe the future of life extension lies in manipulating the genetic blueprint that DNA encodes.

molecules; the stiffening is due to chemical reactions that cause the molecules to form bonds, which prevent the mesh from bending or stretching. Mulling this over, Bjorksten made a startling leap: He proposed that similar bonding, which he called "cross-linkage," must take place in human cells as they grow older. Aging, he proposed, is nothing more than an irreversible set of reactions among the molecules in the body that renders cells incapable of properly going about their daily business.

But Bjorksten's logic had a deeper layer. He placed the blame on a failure of the body's natural defenders against inappropriate bonding between molecules. These defenders, he noted, are enzymes—specialized proteins that constantly roam about and perform a wide range of biochemical housekeeping chores. In the tissues of a youngster, explained Bjorksten, enzymes easily sever most of the cross-links that form between proteins. But enzyme efficiency drops with age, and consequently the number of cells incapacitated by cross-links grows until tissues and even whole organs falter.

Most gerontologists today prefer to view cross-linkage as an effect of aging rather than a cause; presumably, some other force must be acting upon enzymes to weaken them. More and more researchers are suggesting that this malign force is exerted by a class of unstable molecules called free radicals. These are run-of-the-mill compounds that have lost electrons from their outer shells as a result of contact with agents such as radiation, cigarette smoke, or smog, and also as a by-product of an organism's use of oxygen to metabolize food. Free radicals can be a menace in cells, latching on to other molecules to make up for their missing electron. In doing so, they may set off a chain reaction: A single free radical may give rise to a hundred others.

Free radicals can wreak biological havoc in a number of ways. In addition to cross-linkage, the minute provocateurs can split stable molecules or knock pieces off them, creating a sort of chemical garble. They may prod cells to become cancerous, increase the devastation to the heart muscle in the aftermath of a seizure or stroke, encourage the buildup of fats in arteries, hasten cataract formation, and worsen any number of other degenerative ailments.

Denham Harman, a physician and biochemist now at the University of Nebraska School of Medicine in Omaha, was the first to propose that free radicals were the cause of aging. While researching the effects of radiation on mice in the 1950s, Harman discovered that exposure to the toxic rays induces the symptoms of aging and shortens life span. He also determined that radiation causes an enormous increase in the number of free radicals in each cell. Concluding that the free radicals were responsible for the rapid aging of the mice, Harman deduced that if bombardment by the unstable atoms advances the process of growing old, then the natural and gradual accumulation of free radicals in otherwise healthy cells must bring on normal aging.

Harman treated the irradiated mice with antioxidants, substances used in industry to prevent such free-radical damage as the deterioration of leather, rubber, and synthetics. He found that the substances also proved to reverse aging symptoms. Intrigued, the physician tested antioxidants on healthy animals, an experiment that revealed that the substances actually combat free radicals and thus increase a species' average life expectancy. Maximum possible life span, though, remains the same.

As with the specific case of cross-linkage, however, many scientists believe that free-radical damage may be an effect of aging, not the cause. According to the second main school of gerontological thought, aging is not, at root, a consequence of environmental or metabolic slings and arrows, but rather is a result of preordained physiological obsolescence, as if organisms, like grandfather clocks, were wound up only to wind down again. Just as organisms are programmed at birth to grow and develop, so they might be programmed to die. The key to the clock mechanism may lie within the genes or the brain. In either case, if it were possible to halt the pendulum, or to rewind the clock, death might be vanquished.

The Pet with a Gift of Longevity

Sleek and mysterious, the cat has long fascinated humans with its seeming facility to defy death. It plummets from great heights to land on all fours, unharmed. It walks narrow ledges with the skill of a gymnast. It discerns danger in the dark with keen night vision. Such talents have earned it the tantalizing—if erroneous—reputation of having nine lives.

In ancient Egypt, the cat symbolized life itself. It was sacred to Bastet, the life-giving cat goddess who ruled fertility and health. Today, scientists are finding that Egyptians were wise to revere the cat, for recent studies have shown that the animals may indeed bless their masters and

An Egyptian artisan fashioned this bronze cat in about 600 BC. Cats were so sacred they were often mummified after death.

mistresses with longer, happier lives.

Owning a cat—or any pet—can benefit nearly everyone, experts say. People's blood pressure drops when they talk to or stroke a cat. They gain self-esteem and a sense of order providing for a pet's daily needs. Depressed people improve markedly after adopting a kitten. Children grappling with their parents' divorce feel better if they have an animal confidant. Pet owners visit their doctors less often than do people without pets. And people with heart disease actually live longer if they own pets.

For people who live in nursing homes, cats can be particularly therapeutic. In one case, a frail, elderly man refused to eat. The nurses, finding that his sole interest in life was the home's resident kittens, told him he could keep the kittens in his room if he ate. He agreed and gained forty pounds.

Some people have even suggested that cats have an uncanny sense of which people need them most. Out of a room full of senior citizens, for instance, one nursing-home cat singled out a woman who had not spoken for months. Delighted, she immediately broke her silence.

A senior citizen enjoys a book under her cat's calm surveillance. People reportedly enjoy better health if they have pets to care for.

The notion that body cells have a limited life span dates to the late 1950s, when Leonard Hayflick, then a scientist at the Wistar Institute in Philadelphia, discovered that most types of cells in the human body divide only a finite number of times—fifty times on average, sixty at the absolute outside. Previously, it was generally believed that any cell taken out of the body and placed in a nourishing medium, or culture, would go on dividing indefinitely. A few researchers suspected that cultured cells had a finite life span, but Hayflick was the first to prove it beyond doubt. Follow-up studies with lung, skin, muscle, heart, liver, and kidney cells revealed that all would replicate happily for a while, then slow the pace, and finally die, filled with litter spewed from their malfunctioning machinery.

Theorists surmise that the universal failure that ensues when a colony of cells reaches the Hayflick limit, as it has come to be known, is caused by the switching off of critical genes. The behavior of these genes might be compared to workers whose labor contract has expired: Having passed a stipulated deadline, they stage a walkout (in this case, of course, the work stoppage is not temporary but permanent). For a time in the 1970s, it appeared to gerontologists that they had found further support for the genetic hypothesis of aging in the rare and tragic disease called progeria. This wasting malady affects fewer than twenty children throughout the world, turning them into shriveled parodies of the elderly, and usually bringing death by age thirteen. However, although progeria is caused by a genetic flaw, its ravages only superficially resemble those of true

Andrew Da Passano rings a bell to end a meditation, part of an antiaging seminar he teaches in Los Angeles. He claims to renew aging cells through the rituals of Eastern mystics.

aging. Progeria causes no deterioration of the sense organs, nor does it subject victims to common plagues of old age, such as arthritis or mental infirmity.

Although the facts of the Hayflick limit are not in dispute, their meaning is. Hayflick himself does not view the phenomenon as the fundamental reason for death. "Cell division is only one cell process. I don't believe cells or human beings die because cells stop dividing, but from functional changes that occur before cell division stops." Nor is it clear that each cell follows the aging track without outside guidance. Some researchers believe the cells are not responding to their own internal aging timers but instead are heeding the signal of a higher anatomical executioner. A former Harvard biochemist, W. Donner Denckla, argues that the pituitary gland, a tiny kernel in the brain that directs the release of several key hormones, triggers aging. The culprit, says Denckla, is a hypothetical hormone that he has named Decreasing Oxygen Consumption, or DECO—widely referred to among antiaging buffs as the death hormone. No one knows if DECO exists, and Denckla has so far failed in his efforts to extract pure samples of it from human tissues. But he is convinced that it begins circulating in the blood at puberty, starting the body down the path that leads to death.

Physicians are often in the position of having to treat a disease without fully comprehending how it operates inside the body. Perhaps they will learn to counteract the effects of aging despite the gaps in theoretical understanding of it. In casting about for possible weapons, many researchers have

turned their gaze onto the natural world, looking for long-lived species that might employ genetic strategies helpful to *Homo sapiens.* Some species appear to age hardly at all over the course of hundreds or even thousands of years. The massive redwoods of the Pacific Northwest live 3,000 years or more without showing signs of decay. Bristlecone pine trees, which grow in the high desert regions of the American Southwest, can survive almost 5,000 years, adding new cells in years when rainfall is ample and shutting down almost completely in times of drought. Even more venerable are creosote bushes found in southern California: Some are 10,000 years old. Similarly, sponges and sea anemones persist in a kind of suspended animation, living for nearly 100 years without visible signs of deterioration. And colonies of bacteria and yeast can divide for hundreds of years, subject to no Hayflick limit of their own.

Such longevity in the floral and faunal kingdoms may derive from a salutory arrangement of genes, which somehow counteracts or forestalls the withering of age. Working with the nematode, a type of roundworm, investigators at the University of Colorado at Boulder have identified and manipulated at least one gene that is directly related to aging. When they produced a strain of the worm carrying an altered copy of the gene, that strain lived more than twice as long as usual, about fifty-six days as opposed to nineteen. The nematode's age-1 gene, as the scientists named it, is also somehow connected to reproduction, since the worms with the mutated gene produced fewer offspring, falling far short of the 250,000-egg-a-day norm. Perhaps, these researchers speculate, humans also possess a gene or group of genes that could be altered to add years to life.

The best hope for discovering such gerontogenes, if they exist, resides with the Human Genome Project, a proposed mapping of all the genes—an estimated 100,000 of them—that make up the human genetic blueprint. This prospective undertaking by scientists around the world, which might cost as much as three billion dollars and take as long as fifteen years to complete, is favored by a number of prominent biologists. They argue that unraveling the entire genetic code will enable researchers to identify wayward genes responsible for scores of inheritable diseases. Eventually, they say, medicine could learn to replace damaged genes or to excise renegade ones, curing genetic diseases or stopping them before they begin. A further payoff would be insights into aging, for if the process is indeed directed by genes, these would be more easily pinpointed if the entire DNA map were laid out. But the project also has vocal opponents, who feel the monetary resources would be better allocated to other research aims.

Any possible genetic countermand to aging lies far in the future. But a wide spectrum of drug or dietary candidates for an antiaging role—hormones, vitamins, herbs, and more—are very much of the here and now. The claims made for some are highly suspect, but solid science underpins a number of them.

Hormones, known to decline in efficacy and abundance as the body grows older, demonstrate certain powers to stem the tide of aging. Human growth hormone (hGH), a product of the pituitary gland, has been shown to convert flab to muscle and to strengthen bone. In a study completed in 1990, scientists at the Medical College of Wisconsin in Milwaukee gave periodic injections of a synthetic version of this hormone to a dozen older men.

After four months, the men had become leaner, fitter, and, with regard to certain blood factors, downright youthful. Subjects in other similar studies also appeared rejuvenated after courses of human growth hormone, losing wrinkles, flexing newfound muscles, and regaining a long-lost spring in their steps. Concludes Daniel Rudman, professor of medicine at the Medical College and associate chief of staff for extended care at the VA Medical Center in Milwaukee, "Our study showed that six months of hormone treatment reversed one to two decades of aging with regard to body composition."

Perhaps these test subjects are harbingers of a day when hGH is taken in measured daily doses at the breakfast table to guard against aging. For now, though, the public must await a full analysis of the hormone's side effects. Some side effects already known can be life-threatening if hGH is not properly administered. And there is other evidence of the dangers: People who have a natural overabundance of human growth hormone are susceptible to such problems as diabetes, arthritis, and grotesque overdevelopment of facial features and the bones of the hands and feet. Endocrinologist Mary Lee Vance of the University of Virginia cautions, "This hormone is a double-edged sword."

In the search for substances that combat aging, serendipity has sometimes played a role. One example is a prescription drug known

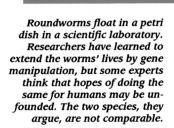

Roundworms float in a petri dish in a scientific laboratory. Researchers have learned to extend the worms' lives by gene manipulation, but some experts think that hopes of doing the same for humans may be unfounded. The two species, they argue, are not comparable.

abroad and in Canada as Deprenyl, and distributed in the United States under the name Eldepryl. Initially targeted against Parkinson's disease, a major neurological ailment, Deprenyl appears to enhance the production of dopamine, an important chemical messenger in the brain that is deficient in victims of Parkinson's.

But the drug's inventor, Joseph Knoll, a Hungarian physician who is a member of his own nation's Academy of Sciences and an honorary member of Britain's Royal Academy of Sciences, believes that Deprenyl has an added talent. In experiments he conducted with rats, he found that the drug lengthened the animals' life spans by 34 percent. So convinced is Knoll that Deprenyl confers longer life that he and his wife both take the drug twice weekly, even though they are healthy. Knoll says the drug improves brain function and also acts as an aphrodisiac—alleged benefits that have made it a much-sought-after commodity in Europe and North America.

Knoll believes Deprenyl could extend the average life expectancy from about 75 years of age to 95. Some other antiaging proponents go so far as to suggest that people taking the drug might live well beyond Knoll's estimate, perhaps to the age of 150. In the United States, Deprenyl is approved by the Food and Drug Administration (FDA) only for use in the treatment of Parkinson's disease. But American doctors may, at their discretion, prescribe the drug for life extension, although few do for fear of malpractice suits.

Another drug that held surprises for its developers is the French-made RU-486, known widely in the United States as the "morning after" abortion pill. Reviled by pro-life groups for its intended purpose, RU-486 seems to have value as a therapeutic drug for breast cancer, hypertension, Alzheimer's disease, and a number of other devastating ailments. The drug also appears to block the release of some hormones that have been linked with aging. Going under the shorthand label of stress hormones, these substances hasten the loss of bone and muscles, and impair the ability of the immune system to attack invading viruses and bacteria or to kill cancerous cells. Gerontologist William Regelson at the Medical College of Virginia hazards that RU-486 may be "the most potent antiaging drug available"—available outside the United States, that is. At present, its import is banned by the FDA.

Dozens of other drugs are reputed to prolong youth.

Some are sold through health and natural-food outlets, some on the gray and black markets. Gerovital, for instance, is a blend of the local anesthetic procaine (a chemical cousin to cocaine) and fillers. The recipe belongs to Ana Aslan, a Romanian physician who claims the mixture gives those who take it smoother, wrinkle-free skin, greater strength, and increased powers of recall. Other drugs said to have antiaging properties are AL-721, a fatty compound found in egg yolks; DHEA, a hormone prevalent in the blood of young adults but rarely found in that of the elderly; L059, a drug under testing in Europe that may improve alertness and the ability to think and reason; and Phenformin, an antibiotic that seems to stimulate lagging immune systems.

Many herbal remedies are also being examined for possible rejuvenating action. Chinese ginseng root, for instance, contains the trace element germanium, which has been shown to relieve symptoms of arthritis and heart disease. And quinones, a group of compounds found in fruits, vegetables, and yeast-fermented foods such as yogurt and beer, may counteract free radicals, quashing the destructive molecules on contact. Quinones occur naturally in the body, but their level can be boosted, possibly reducing the free-radical damage involved in aging.

The same antioxidants that Denham Harman used in the 1950s to treat his irradiated mice have also been held up as antiaging panaceas for humans. Vitamin E, for one, has long been touted by assorted diet and fitness gurus for its supposed antiaging benefits. In the 1970s, best-selling nutrition author Adelle Davis sang the praises of vitamin E, and Americans began gobbling the supplement. Even NASA astronauts were dosed with vitamin E, preflight, to counteract the rigors of living in oxygen-rich space capsules. Advocates cited it as a sure route to everything from better-looking skin to more robust hearts and renewed sexual potency. While its efficacy as a sex vitamin has been disproved, the promising results of recent international research has led Jeffrey Blumberg, associate director of the Human Nutrition Research Center on Aging at Boston's Tufts University, to comment, "Today, we're on safe ground

when we talk about using vitamin E to help prevent some of the diseases that come with age."

Linus Pauling, a brilliant and iconoclastic two-time Nobel laureate, claimed even more sweeping powers for vitamin C. Pauling had become interested in vitamin C research after reading the work of New Jersey biochemist Irwin Stone, who pointed out that, unlike humans, most animals manufacture large amounts of vitamin C. Stone reasoned that humans would live healthier—and perhaps longer—lives if they consumed supplements to bolster the vitamin's presence in the body. "His arguments were so rational to a scientist that I just had to accept them," Pauling recalled in a 1991 *Washington Post* interview.

Since then, ninety-year-old Pauling and his followers have advocated taking megadoses of the vitamin, claiming that it strengthens the immune system and helps to avert or control numerous ailments—the common cold, flu, hepatitis, cardiovascular disease, cancer, and even schizophrenia. Moreover, vitamin C is said to delay the process of aging. Although Pauling has been pilloried within the scientific community, he stands by his claims. And research continues that may someday validate his beliefs. "Because his claims are so strong, people found them hard to believe and tended to dismiss them," explains epidemiologist Gladys Block of the University of California at Berkeley. "The world is catching up with him."

The world may take longer to catch up with Durk Pearson and Sandy Shaw, a California husband and wife who came up with their own ideas about aging in 1982, in their book *Life Extension: A Practical Scientific Approach.* They have been widely criticized by the scientific establishment, which points out that they hold only bachelor's degrees—his in physics, hers in chemistry. They formulated their notions about aging through a wide-ranging program of reading. Their advice, in sum, is do not worry about fat, calories, or exercise, but be sure to ingest special concoctions—devised by them—of vitamins, minerals, and other

French chemist Étienne Baulieu exhibits a tablet of RU-486, the drug that he and his research team developed. He says the pill—which is now prescribed outside the United States to induce abortion—could also serve as "a preventive medicine for increasing life span."

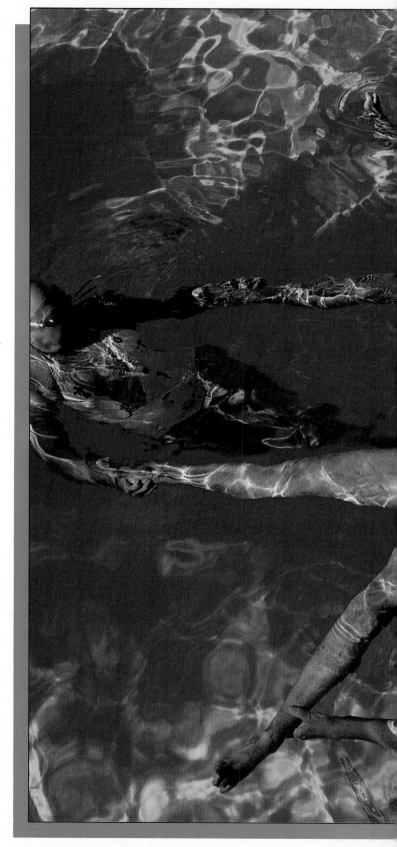

Women, like these swimming in a retirement-community pool, tend to outlive men by nearly seven years. Research has credited genetic differences and women's wider circles of friends.

supposedly valuable substances. The pamphlets for their line of products, including such items as Fast Blast and PowerMaker II nutrient drinks, are filled with references to quick, lasting energy, high performance, and brain food.

Chief among Pearson and Shaw's products is one they developed in 1968 and have been refining ever since. Called Personal Radical Shield formula, a reference to the free radical theory of aging, the mixture contains thirteen vitamins, beta carotene, chromium, copper, iodine, manganese, molybdenum, selenium, zinc, and other ingredients. The couple take it four times a day; in fact, they typically dose themselves with some type of supplement a dozen times daily. Claiming that they cannot afford the expense of double-blind studies, Pearson and Shaw substitute self-experimentation for established research protocol, a fact that clearly riles the majority of medical antiaging experts. "They are marketing gurus who want to turn everyone into a modern-day chemistry experiment," opined John Renner, a physician and president of the Consumer Health Research Information Institute in Kansas City, Missouri, in a 1990 interview. "That is not the way science ought to work."

For all of Pearson and Shaw's apparent success—theirs is a million-dollar business, and they count film star Clint Eastwood among their loyal customers—the claims made for diet supplements leave most mainstream scientists cold. Far more exciting to serious researchers are the emerging facts about diet restriction—the huge increases in life span achieved by feeding animals only 60 percent of their normal caloric intake. The notion that dietary restraint can prolong life is far from new, as evidenced by the sixteenth-century Venetian Luigi Cornaro, who credited meager portions of food and drink with allowing him to live a full and vigorous life until his death at age ninety-eight. And for generations familiar homilies have proclaimed the virtues of moderation at the table—"feed sparingly and defy the physician," for example, or "he that eats but one dish seldom needs the doctor." But systematic efforts to determine the relationship

of aging and abstemiousness are only a few decades old. Leading the way, beginning in the late 1920s, was biologist Clive McCay of Cornell University.

McCay conducted experiments first with trout and then for many years with rats, feeding some animals a standard lab diet and others a low-calorie one supplemented with vitamins and minerals. Repeated studies showed that although a shortage of calories in the developmental phase of the rats' lives stunted their growth, they lived much longer—about 1,400 days versus just less than 1,000 for the control animals. Translated into human terms, this meant that they reached about 150 years of age.

The two groups of rats showed marked differences in their physical conditions. The free-eating rats grew weak and sluggish, and their fur became dull and matted. Some showed signs of deteriorating hearts or kidneys; others developed tumors or diabetes or cataracts. But the calorie-restricted rats appeared almost unaffected by the passage of time. Nearing the end of the typical life span, they remained bright-eyed and vigorous. Their fur was lustrous, and they could move more quickly than their better-fed laboratory cousins. They showed no signs of illness and indeed remained almost entirely free of disease until their deaths. Some, in fact, retained such excellent health at the end of their lives that the cause of death was unclear.

Follow-up studies undertaken by other investigators in the 1960s reaffirmed McCay's findings—and added a few interesting sidelights. A 1961 experiment demonstrated that while the life-extending effects of diet restriction were greatest when the calorie cut was instituted early in life, they were significant even if animals were fed normally to begin with, then later shifted onto a low-calorie regime.

Another sort of dietary restriction prompted a 1963 edition of the tabloid *National Enquirer* to blare, "YOU WILL LIVE FOREVER." The paper claimed that top-secret government research had already unlocked the mystery of eternal youth, which was being withheld from the citizenry due to its explosive nature. In fact, the study in question had been carried out under the auspices of the Monsanto Corporation

The Healing Powers of a Pungent Bulb

A Philadelphia scientist will never forget a sixty-six-year-old woman he once met: She looked only forty-four and acted as spry as a twenty-two-year-old. She attributed her remarkable youthfulness to a clove of garlic in her nightly salad.

She may have been correct. For millennia, garlic has been a favorite folk prescription for a host of ills and seemingly for good reason. Recent scientific studies have revealed that the lowly stinking rose, as it is sometimes jokingly known, lowers the amount of fat in the bloodstream. It also reduces the clotting of blood in the arteries. Both of these effects may decrease one's chances of suffering heart attack or stroke.

Furthermore, preliminary studies have shown that garlic may help prevent certain cancers. It is an antioxidant, offering the human body protection from free radicals, the carcinogenic molecules produced by radiation and toxins in the environment.

Because many people shy away from the herb because of its strong odor, a few companies market supposedly odor-free garlic capsules, though scientists disagree on the efficacy of these supplements and on the amount of garlic that may be beneficial.

A dapper Victorian vampire busses a young lady. It was once thought that wearing garlic deterred such advances.

Concealing their health-enhancing properties within, shiny white bulbs of garlic adorn braided garlands of straw.

by their director of research, scientist Richard Gordon, and while it amplified understanding of undernutrition, it was by no means the world-shaking piece of work the *Enquirer* claimed. Gordon had focused on just one essential nutrient, the amino acid tryptophan, present in many foods and used by the body to assemble proteins. Deprived almost completely of tryptophan, chickens and mice in Gordon's lab markedly slowed their maturation and were thrown into a kind of prolonged adolescence.

Intrigued by Gordon's efforts, Paul Segall, an ardent, young biologist with a spotty college record, decided to carry out similar antiaging studies of his own. On an ad hoc basis, he commenced a series of undernutrition experiments, first at the University of Pittsburgh, then in a makeshift lab in the garage of his Long Island home, and finally at the University of California at Berkeley, where he eventually earned a Ph.D. In his tests, rats were fed diets low in tryptophan and were then subjected to assorted stresses, such as being plunged into ice water. Compared to a control group of rats on a normal diet, the low-tryptophan subjects weathered the stresses impressively. In time, Segall realized that the less tryptophan the rats ingested, the longer their life span. He noted that rats with a restricted intake also remained fecund far longer than normal; one thirty-three-

month-old female produced pups, which Segall equated with an eighty-year-old woman delivering a child. Unfortunately, most people will probably never enjoy the apparent benefits of a tryptophan-reduced diet; restricting the amino acid in humans leads to severe side effects, including death.

Perhaps the leading American exponent of the possibilities of undernutrition—the caloric kind—is UCLA gerontologist Roy Walford. He has an evolutionary explanation for the results seen in restricted-diet experiments, attributing them to a natural mechanism that enables animals to survive protracted periods of scarcity caused by drought and other environmental calamities. Walford suspects that such naturally imposed curtailment of caloric intake prompts a diminishment of activity at the cellular level. "When the animals consume less, they have less energy available overall. To survive, they must redirect what energy remains, which would normally be spent on such activities as rapid reproduction, growth and cell division, and channel it into maintenance and repair of cells and tissues. This extends the period of youthfulness."

The benefits of caloric restriction for larger animals are just beginning to be

Self-taught life-extension gurus Durk Pearson and Sandy Shaw sit within easy reach of their supposedly antiaging products. The supplements have not been tested scientifically for effectiveness, but the couple take them daily.

sounded, but some gerontologists are sufficiently impressed by the evidence in hand to extrapolate to humans. Walford, for one, has put himself on a diet similar in concept to those that have yielded such marked prolongation of life in the lab. For most of his adult life, he consumed about 2,500 calories a day, but since 1985, he has dropped to a mere 1,500 to 2,000 calories a day—a reduction that has caused him to slowly, steadily lose pounds, bringing his weight down about 25 percent in all. "I don't go by calories, I go by weight," he says. "For humans, I think the reduction should be between 10 and 25 percent— toward the lower end if you are already slender and toward the upper end if you are obese. This means a restriction of calorie intake of around 20 to 30 percent."

The weight loss should not be sudden. "If you translate the animal data to people," says Walford, "the best, safest way to lose the weight is very gradually, over a period of four to six years. In the earlier experiments, where adult animals were put abruptly on a lower-calorie diet, it actually shortened the life span. Quick-loss diets are probably life-shortening—even good ones." When Walford began his weight-reduction program, which emphasizes foods low in fat and high in nutrients, he was 60 years old. He believes that a low-calorie diet will extend his life expectancy to about 120 years.

Although no large-scale, controlled studies have been made of undernutrition in humans, and thus no scientifically acceptable proof of its efficacy exists, Walford contends that population studies bear out his approach. The ethnic Japanese living on the island of Okinawa, for example, eat differently from their counterparts on the mainland, sticking mainly to fish and vegetables, and avoiding salt and sugar. This menu closely matches Walford's plan. Okinawans live to reach 100 years of age at a rate forty times higher than that of mainland Japanese, and this with a total caloric intake of 40 percent less than the average Tokyo resident.

A far more radical strategy against aging would be to stimulate the body to employ its own ability for self-repair

A brittle starfish regenerates its missing fifth arm (top of picture) on a California beach. Although only simple animals are able to restore lost body parts, some experts predict that scientific advances will one day allow organisms as complex as humans to do so.

on the bodily substances called growth factors, which oversee the day-to-day repairs within cells. Purified and administered as drugs, growth factors have worked wonders in cancer patients, victims of severe burns, and recipients of transplants.

In the future, growth factors might prod cells taken from a person's heart, say, to grow into a completely new organ while suspended in a nourishing preparation in a laboratory vessel. The organ—a perfect copy of the body's original—could then be transplanted into the cell donor without risk of rejection, the all-out assault by the immune system that thwarts a large proportion of transplants. The first steps toward this futuristic goal have already been taken in clinics worldwide with the study of patients who have had parts of their livers removed. Unique among the organs, the liver can regrow itself, even if all but a small portion has been excised. An unidentified chemical in the blood apparently gives liver cells the signal to rebuild the missing matter.

In another area, orthopedists have had luck prompting certain cells to form both cartilage and bone by bathing them in a solution containing a special protein. If the growth is halted after a week, the cells form the softer skeletal component; if after ten days, the harder one. Another procedure, electrical stimulation of sheared, split, or unformed bone, also prompts the bone to grow. Add to these skills knowledge of how to regenerate nerves, blood vessels, and tissues, and it becomes possible that whole limbs could be shaped by the physicians of tomorrow.

Finally, and most daringly, researchers could triumph over aging by seeding individuals with the cells to replace deteriorating brains. Already, neurologists are claiming moderate success in delaying the progression of Parkinson's disease by transplanting fetal brain cells into the brains of those ravaged by the disease. The fetal cells are not yet differentiated—that is, they have not developed the

in such a way that whole organs could regenerate.

Although this scenario comes directly from science fiction, it is more than an imaginative fancy—and not necessarily linked to aging. Some biologists expect to see a day when humans mimic starfish and frogs, growing new digits on limbs to replace those lost to accident or amputation.

At least since the eighteenth century, the curious ability of some species to regrow missing appendages has intrigued scientists. The Italian naturalist Lazzaro Spallanzani pondered the frog and the salamander in 1768 and concluded that the ability to regenerate limbs could in theory be acquired by other species. Attention today is concentrated special characteristics that qualify them for particular tasks. These undifferentiated cells fuse with the gray matter and develop into the specialized brain cells called neurons. The new cells are free of the problems of dopamine deficiency that cause Parkinson's. Since many other brain disorders also result from neuronal shortcomings, brain-cell transplants are being discussed as a multipurpose treatment for senility, degenerative genetic ailments such as Huntington's chorea, and even the trauma of stroke or head injury.

Like limb or heart regeneration in humans, visions of brain-mending are speculative. But it has been argued by Willem Kolff, a professor of medicine and surgery at the University of Utah, that lack of money is the biggest hurdle to the cloning of body parts. (Strictly speaking, cloning is the creation of a new organism without the mechanism of sexual reproduction and from a single parent rather than two. But the term has also come to be used for growing parts of an organism from cells of a parent organism.) If the government allocated a larger share of the biomedical research funds to studies on organ replacement, he maintains, the technology might be made available in as little as a decade. In the twenty-first century, the procedure may become as routine as heart surgery. Some scientists say it probably would be much easier to clone an entire human being than separate body parts. Biologist Paul Segall, for one, points out that "in nature each organ grows in what amounts to a biological field"—that is, in the body.

He believes "it would be very difficult to clone separate organs" without feedback from the rest of the anatomy.

So Segall suggests there will come a day when whole human bodies—rendered insentient early in the fetal stage—are grown from cloned cells to provide living organ banks for their originators. The process, he says, might work like this. First, a few skin cells would be scraped from the person desiring to be cloned. The nucleus from one of the cells, which contains all the genetic information necessary to manufacture every other cell type in the body, would be inserted into an egg cell from which the nucleus had been removed. The egg would grow in a culture medium until it develops to the early embryonic stage, when it would then be transplanted into the womb of a chimpanzee, or an artificial womb.

About six weeks along, a technician skilled in microsurgery would take the fetus from the womb and extract the

A medic rushes a donor heart from an airplane to an ambulance en route to a hospital. There, a deathly ill patient is being prepared to receive the vital organ, which promises him the hope for a longer life.

knot of cells that otherwise would grow into the higher brain. Without those cells, the organism could "never develop into a conscious, feeling human being," says Segall, but instead would remain a "human-looking vegetable." The brain cells could be frozen and used at some future time to rejuvenate aging neurons of the original donor's brain. The fetus, meanwhile, would be reimplanted, and would continue to develop until being delivered by Cesarean section. For a year or two afterward, the clone would be sustained on supernutrients and given hormone injections to ensure proper growth. Finally, the fresh organs and tissues could be harvested from the clone and transplanted into the donor, restoring him or her to youthfulness.

Upon first reading, Segall admits, the whole idea of a living but brainless human serving as an organ bank may seem repugnant, especially if the ultimate goal of cloning is

merely a selfish desire on the donor's part to extend his or her life indefinitely or to look and feel young far beyond the time nature intended. "Is this a blueprint for the future," Segall asks rhetorically, "or a horror movie?"

However, he also envisions instances where cloned body parts could save lives, even very young lives. In his 1989 book on the subject, *Living Longer, Growing Younger,*

Two fetuses (above) share a single umbilical cord in their mother's uterus in a computer-enhanced ultrasound image. Identical twins, such as these and the nine-year-old boys pictured at left, form when one fertilized egg splits, creating two individuals that are exactly alike. At least one cloning expert believes that future technology could allow a single fetus to be replicated—with controversial implications. The cloned embryo, he says, would be frozen and stored as a potential organ donor. If the original person ever needed a new body part, the clone might be allowed to develop to fill the bill.

Cloned calves huddle together, each distinguished from the others by a numbered ear tag. Scientists created the animals by uniting cow eggs and cells from bovine embryos, and some experts think that soon humans could be produced in similar fashion.

he offers a hypothetical example of a little girl involved in a tragic accident that burns most of her skin and damages her lungs beyond repair. She is made whole and happy again by transplants from a clone her parents prudently agreed to pay for when she was born. Replacement organs from a body clone could be considered a type of "life insurance," says Segall, to be called upon when one's very existence is hanging in the balance. He suggests that it might become almost routine for families who could afford it to have one or two clone-standbys created for each child at birth, to be stored for use in case of devastating accident or illness.

Many people want no part of the future as foreseen by Segall. Andrew Kimbrell, policy director of the Foundation on Economic Trends, told writer Bill Lawren that "a grisly Brave New World" could be the result of such practices. "Our society has a reverence for the human body that's in-trinsic to our whole concept of human rights," Kimbrell said. "If we get into the business of creating human bodies that are nothing but brain-dead organ repositories, it could damage our view of the human body as sacred." Many physicians and other medical workers, no doubt, would refuse to take part in removing the brain cells from a living fetus. Some thoughtful people object, too, to the basic idea of manipulating genes in any way.

Presumably the cloned fetus could be allowed to grow and develop normally, as described in David Rorvik's book about Max, thus creating a thinking, feeling genetic duplicate of the skin cell donor. Although a judge called Rorvik's account a hoax, the concept cannot be entirely dismissed, since scientists have indeed cloned many other species.

Technically, the simplest form of cloning is the cleaving of a single bacterium to produce two genetically

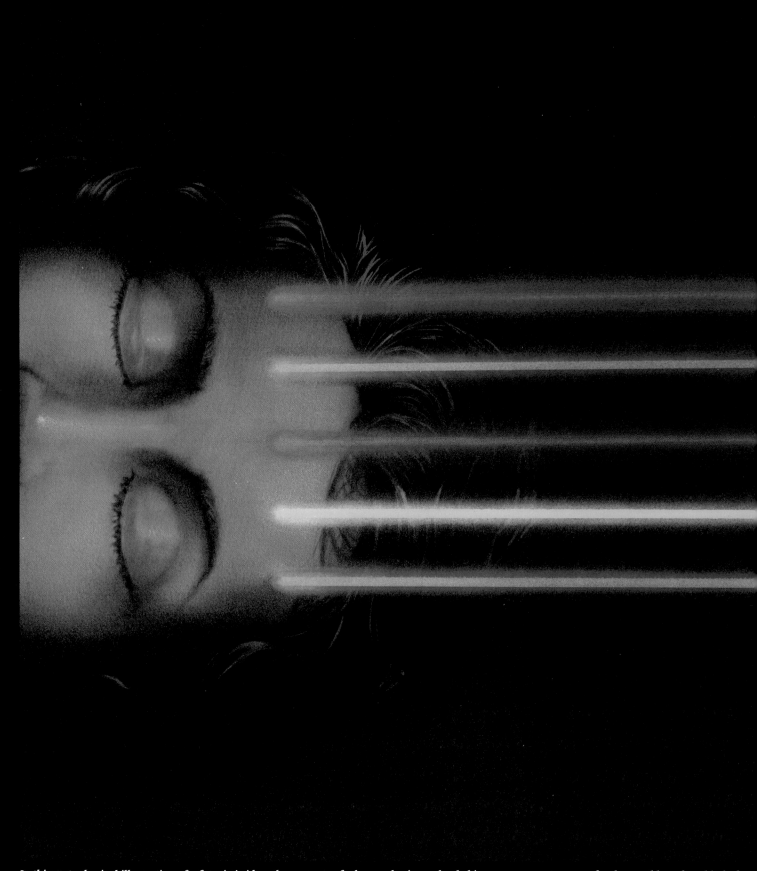

In this metaphorical illustration of a futuristic idea, the contents of a human brain are loaded into a computer—a transfer that could confer a kind of

identical bacteria. Many botanical species can be cloned by root division: Blueberries, daylilies, and other plants are propagated in this fashion. Most plants can now also be cloned in the laboratory from single cells.

When scientists speak of cloning animals, they mean, again, genetically copying the organism. Nature sometimes does this on its own: Identical twins can be thought of as naturally produced clones of a sort. During the 1980s, researchers made great leaps that enabled them to artificially split single, fertilized egg cells of mice, rabbits, calves, and horses to produce identical offspring. But performing the same trick with humans will take time, resources in the billions of dollars, and, many commentators feel, should be carried out only after a thorough public discussion of its ethical implications—if at all.

Should antiaging research fail entirely in its quest for organic means to extend life, those on the trail of Shangri-la might turn to robotic devices. After all, computers have already been programmed to imitate networks of human brain cells, to play chess, and to make decisions. While these imitative skills are still rudimentary, many researchers contend that, in a matter of a few decades, so-called artificial intelligence will outstrip the human variety. When that happens, says Carnegie Mellon University computer scientist Hans Moravec, the world will enter a postbiological age "dominated by self-improving, thinking machines."

Moravec, who began building robots as a ten-year-old, is exhilarated by this possibility, claiming to have "no loyalty to DNA." In his 1988 book titled *Mind Children: The Future of Robot and Human Intelligence,* he outlines a method for transferring the contents of a human brain into a computer. A surgeon would hook up a computer and a small section of the brain via electrodes. The surgeon would then stimulate that part of the brain and monitor it until the computer could take over its function. That part of the human brain would then be destroyed, and another section copied into the computer—and so on, until the entire contents of the brain were transferred.

Then the computer, bearing all the memories and con-

sciousness of the original individual, could be installed in a robot. By the time all this is possible, Moravec predicts, the primitive robots of the 1970s will have evolved into full-fledged cybernetic species able to roam the universe at will. Just as space probes have explored moons and planets throughout the Solar System, twenty-first-century robots could venture deep into the galaxy, discovering new wonders with the aid of a human consciousness electronically imprinted in their memories.

This version of immortality is perhaps not what most people have in mind when they think of extending their stay on the planet. Quipped a *Wall Street Journal* headline for an article describing Moravec's vision, "Good News: You Can Live Forever; Bad News: No Sex." Some critics have termed the scheme a manifestation of supreme hubris—blasphemous pride. Moravec himself considers it highly altruistic. He foresees a time when humans will step aside altogether, discarding their corruptible flesh for eminently reparable machine bodies. "This evolutionary process" of conveying human consciousness into robotic replacements "means that we are already immortal, as we have been since the dawn of life," he writes. Cybernetic offspring would continue the human adventure, passing on culture from one generation to the next. Moravec's dream may seem utterly farfetched and improbable. But as he likes to point out, so did space travel at the beginning of the twentieth century.

But for most who ponder the subject of physical immortality, the goal is not to spend eternity as a machine, but to enjoy an endless, youthful biological life. Cardiologist Lawrence Lamb contemplates the potential benefits for human civilization as a whole: "The opportunity for great minds to live, experience, and create offers fantastic possibilities. What contributions to society could Leonardo da Vinci, with his inventive genius, not have made, in a world that had electricity, engines, new sources of power, if he had lived in a state of youthful being for 500 years." And as to the likelihood of it coming to pass, Lamb is confident. *"What can happen will happen,"* he declares, "and immortality can and will happen."

Battling the Ravages of Time

Immortality may be desired by many, but few are willing to spend eternity growing ever more wrinkled and infirm. Thus it is that the quest for eternal life is inextricably bound up with the quest for eternal youth.

Down through the ages, smooth skin, thick, lustrous hair, and well-toned muscles have been associated with fertility, virility, and power—the hallmarks of an individual in the prime of life. Julius Caesar, for one, is said to have worn his signature laurel wreath in an effort to camouflage his balding pate. And in Renaissance Europe, Henri de Mondeville, chief surgeon to King Philip IV of France, addressed what he deemed "the irreversible outrage of the years" by prescribing such drastic treatments as slicing off slack facial skin with a razor blade.

In his 1300 treatise entitled "Cyrurgie"—or "surgery"—Mondeville also described makeup, depilatories, hair dye, soaps, and drugs that allegedly rejuvenated the user's appearance. All have a familiar ring in modern times, when cosmetics, cosmetic surgery, and weight loss are multimillion-dollar industries.

The photographs on the following pages reveal how people of many cultures and many eras have sought remedies for or safeguards against the physical ravages of time. Some of the treatments, such as the hair-growth stimulator shown above, are now known to be worthless, although they were heartily embraced in their day. Others, such as protecting skin from the sun, do in fact help to preserve some of the bloom of youth.

How to Maintain That Schoolgirl Glow

In ancient Egypt, women crushed incense cakes, wax, and cypress into olive oil and milk, creating a lotion believed to erase wrinkles. Today, cosmetic makers mass-produce moisturizers—and masks, soaps, and makeup—that consumers buy with similar hopes. But according to scientists, such products merely affect the epidermis, the outermost layer of the skin; at best, they remove dead skin cells or briefly plump wrinkles with moisture to make them less visible. The key to permanent wrinkle removal lies in a deeper layer of skin, the dermis. The drug Retin-A has shown some promise as an antiaging formula, but the U.S. government has yet to approve it.

According to this 1940 French advertisement, the beauty cream Diadermine provides twenty-four-hour skin protection by creating an invisible screen against face-ravaging onslaughts of the environment.

A fresh-faced young woman holds a suitor transfixed by the sweetness of her countenance in this 1920s advertisement for Palmolive soap. The slogan— "Keep that schoolgirl complexion"—promised that regular use of the product maintained one's youthful good looks.

This makeup kit, once used by a lady of the Roman Empire, might serve as well today. The jar for rouge, the palette for mixing colors, and the variety of applicators differ little from their modern counterparts, suggesting the tools for beauty, like the quest, are ageless.

Her hair protected by a pink cloth, a visitor to the Montecatini Spa in central Italy allows a mud mask to work its magic by drying upon her face. The natural preparation clears away dead layers of skin, leaving a fresher and supposedly younger-looking complexion.

A woman of the Caucasian Kalash people of Afghanistan and Pakistan wears a traditional makeup derived from boiled goat hoofs. The cosmetic is said to defend the skin against the aging effects of cold and sun, a concern addressed elsewhere with a variety of sunscreens.

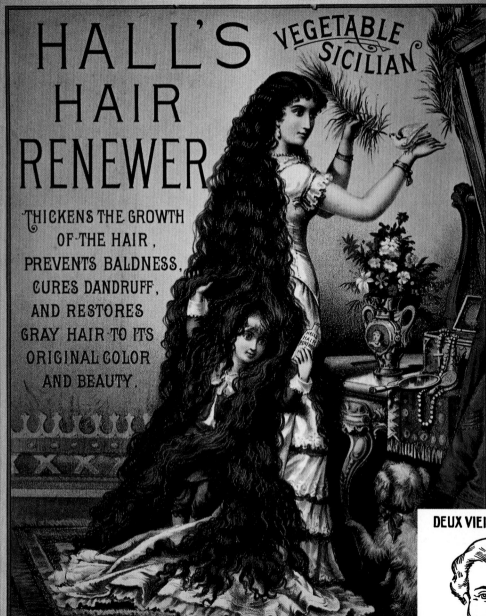

HALL'S HAIR RENEWER

VEGETABLE SICILIAN

THICKENS THE GROWTH OF THE HAIR, PREVENTS BALDNESS, CURES DANDRUFF, AND RESTORES GRAY HAIR TO ITS ORIGINAL COLOR AND BEAUTY.

R.P. HALL & CO. PROPRIETORS, NASHUA, N.H.

Lost in his mother's lush cascade of hair, a little boy attests to the effectiveness of Hall's Hair Renewer, a product that this late-nineteenth-century poster touts as a cure-all for various hair complaints, ranging from dandruff to baldness.

An early before-and-after advertisement extols two French hair products: Niger, for men, and Sublimior, for women. Both tonics supposedly restored color—and hence more youthful appearance—to graying hair.

DEUX VIEILLES MARQUES QUI RAJEUNISSENT !!..

NIGER, SUBLIMIOR

En vente chez tous les coiffeurs, parfumeurs, pharmaciens & herboristes
et à la

PARFUMERIE ROYALE
13, RUE DE TRÉVISE - PARIS

qui vous enverra franco sur demande tarif et notice explicative

Defending the Crowning Glory

"Samson told Delilah all his heart and said unto her, 'There hath not come a razor upon mine head: if I be shaven, then my strength will go from me, and I shall become weak.'" Samson's powerlessness upon losing his hair to Delilah's shears is a theme that has resonated ever since.

For many men, hair loss symbolizes the decline of youthful strength and virility. Nearly all men lose at least some of their hair in a phenomenon called male pattern baldness, which can begin anytime after puberty. For women, the issue is more often graying and thinning hair, but for both sexes, heredity determines which hairs will eventually fall out.

In this ancient wall painting, Egyptian women attending a banquet wear wigs—which indicate high social standing—topped with cones of perfumed wax. Over the course of the evening, the herb-impregnated headdresses would melt, sweetly scenting the wearers' hair.

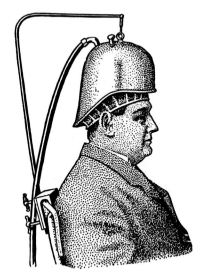

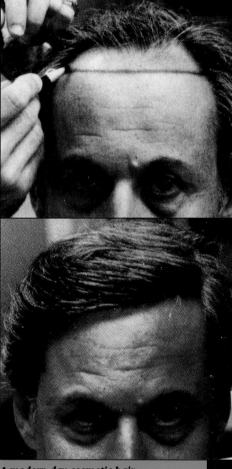

A modern-day cosmetic hair surgeon traces a new hairline on a balding man's scalp (top). Hair from the back and sides of the head will be transplanted to hair follicles in the area of baldness. The result (above) is permanent growth of healthy hair where once there was none.

In an earlier treatment for male baldness, the man in this American advertisement from the late 1800s endures mechanical stimulation of his scalp by the Evans Vacuum Cap. Though unsuccessful, the cap was intended to encourage hair growth by improving the circulation on the top of the head.

Jane Fonda (in pink leotard) leads an exercise class in a dance workout that she choreographed. The actress launched a successful second career as an aerobics instructor when she was nearing middle age, believing physical activity and good nutrition to be the most healthful ways to remain youthful.

With her eyes protected against the intense light, a woman undergoes laser treatment to remove an unsightly mark from her face. The beam stimulates the production of collagen—a natural protein present in young skin—which causes the flaw to vanish permanently.

Schemes for Keeping the Body Beautiful

Faced with slackening skin and thickening waistlines, those approaching middle age have longed to regain their youthful bodies—or even to improve on them. Many find that moderate physical exercise, a sensible diet, and a positive attitude can help them not only to stay healthy but to look younger well into old age. Others feel the need to take more radical steps.

A number of middle-aged people exercise and limit their food intake much more than medical guidelines recommend. And hundreds of thousands of Americans have resorted to cosmetic surgery to create what they consider a more appealing look.

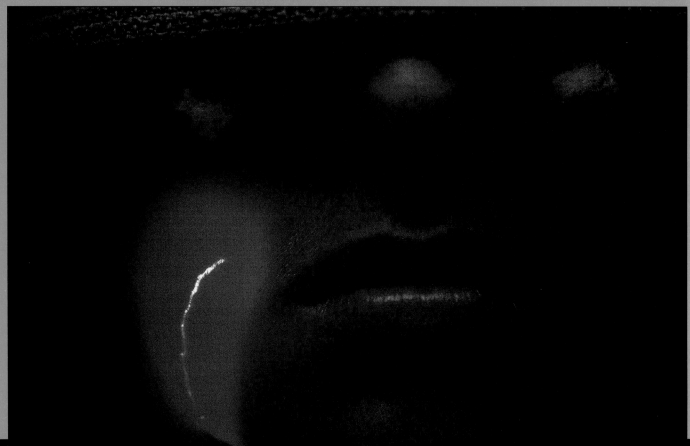

After undergoing a face- and eyelift, a woman displays a photo of her former visage. The cosmetic surgery tautened slack skin and removed many wrinkles, but less drastic measures—hair coloring, removal of eyeglasses, and makeup—also contributed to the woman's more attractive appearance.

A merchant on the streets of the city of Bangalore in southern India peddles a magical elixir that supposedly gives men hulking, muscular physiques such as the ones depicted in the photographs in front of the stand. Prospective buyers may wonder why the vendor himself chooses to remain so slender.

A 1910 French advertisement promises that Doctor Monteil's apparatuses will render the wearer "eternally beautiful and forever young." The rubber Goddess girdle (above) supposedly slimmed the hips and abdomen; facial devices (above, left) fought wrinkles, jowls, crow's feet, and double chins.

95

CHAPTER 3

Dreams Frozen for the Future

The petition that forty-six-year-old Thomas Donaldson presented to a California court in April 1990 based its plea on two irrefutable facts: Donaldson had an incurable brain tumor, and he believed he did not have to die because of it. Although twentieth-century medicine offered no means of eradicating the cancer that was slowly destroying his brain, Donaldson, a computer scientist and mathematician, was convinced that in a few centuries scientists would be able to cure him. The problem he confronted was how to take advantage of a remedy that would not be developed for many decades—long after the tumor could be expected to cause his death.

As the legal brief explained, Donaldson believed he had come up with a practical, if Frankensteinian, solution: He wanted a team of technicians to lower his body temperature while he was still alive, then sever his chilled head and store it in a canister immersed in liquid nitrogen. If or when future technology made it possible not only to cure cancer but also to perform brain transplants and to clone the human form, Donaldson's brain would be thawed, repaired, and placed in a new body grown from his own cells. Revived from his icy state of existence and revitalized with a disease-free brain and a healthy body, Donaldson could then resume his life, albeit in a world much different from the one he had known centuries earlier. But before his brain could go into cold storage, Donaldson needed the court's assurance that those who helped to freeze him would not be subject to criminal prosecution for abetting a suicide.

Cryonic suspension, the controversial process of freezing and storing bodies for later revival, has been practiced since the late 1960s. Ordinarily, however, people are placed in cryonic suspension only after they are pronounced legally dead. Donaldson argued that he could not afford to wait that long. He wanted to be frozen while he was still alive, before the spreading tumor ravaged his brain irretrievably. "I'm sure it would be possible to bring back someone who looks like me, and might be told about many of the things I've done," he told the *Washington Post.* "But so much would be destroyed that it wouldn't really be me. I'm in my brain."

Unconvinced by that line of reasoning, the court on December 27,

1990, ruled against Donaldson's claim. Any California firm that honored his request, the court found, would be violating state law by assisting him to commit suicide, since cryonic suspension clearly qualifies as death under California Health Department regulations. Undaunted, Donaldson filed an appeal in June 1991, determined to press on for what he believed was his only chance to survive.

Suspended animation—as the long-term storage of dormant humans is generally known—has been a topic of scientific speculation since the beginning of the modern era. In 1773, the American statesman and scientist Benjamin Franklin wrote that he wished scientists could "invent a method of embalming drowned persons, in such a manner that they might be recalled to life at any period, however distant." Unfortunately, Franklin added, he lived "in a century too little advanced, and too near the infancy of science, to see such art brought in our time to its perfection."

Since Franklin's day, a number of research breakthroughs have suggested to some that science indeed may be inching toward such a process, most probably through the use of extreme cold. Developments in the freezing and revival of living cells and tissues have enabled scientists to preserve relatively simple forms of biological matter for years or even decades. Studies of hibernating animals have shown that some frogs and turtles routinely survive for days or weeks with much of their bodies frozen solid. In the laboratory, scientists have succeeded in reviving hamsters after short periods in which portions of their body fluids apparently turned to ice. And emergency medical techniques have enabled doctors to revive some human accident victims whose core body temperatures have plunged a chilling ten degrees or more.

Based on these and other scientific studies, enthusiasts such as Donaldson have concluded that cryonic suspension is already a reasonable alternative to death. More than thirty believers have taken the plunge, having been frozen in whole or in part shortly after their legal demise. Hundreds of others still living have expressed interest in the plan. Most scientists, however, are not so optimistic. With medical technicians as yet unable to sustain an organ donor's heart or liver for more than a few hours, the long-term preservation of an organism as extraordinarily complicated as the human body, or an organ as complex as the human brain, remains in the majority view a distant dream.

Conventional science does offer a variation on the cool cure, though, based on experiments in which fish kept in relatively chilly water lived twice as long as warm fish. By lowering body temperatures a few degrees under carefully controlled circumstances, some scientists contend, disease-free human beings may be able to extend their conscious life span to 140 years or more. As for cryonic suspension itself, the theoretical possibility cannot be ruled out. Most of the scientists sympathetic to the idea, however, believe that a reliable freezing and thawing process is unlikely to be perfected in the lifetime of anyone now living.

The myths and legends of myriad cultures tell of human beings sleeping away the decades. In ancient Greek myth, the shepherd boy Epimenides fell asleep for fifty-seven years while searching for a lost sheep; in the Norse sagas, the

Technicians at Alcor Life Extension Foundation remove the foil-wrapped body of James Bedford from an old cylindrical freezer for transfer to a newer model in 1991, about twenty-four years after Bedford became the first human frozen for later revival. Alcor saved Bedford from defrosting after a series of other cryonic suspension companies that held him ceased operations. Mathematician Thomas Donaldson (below), who sued for permission to have Alcor cut off and freeze his head before a brain tumor could kill him, said he saw the procedure as "the only alternative to death."

Valkyrie Brunhilda slumbered inside a circle of fire until she was awakened by Siegfried, the only man brave enough to pierce the flames. The princess Sleeping Beauty, heroine of the seventeenth-century French fairy tale, dozed for 100 years before a prince revived her with a kiss. Nineteenth-century American author Washington Irving brought the theme to modern times with the tale of Rip Van Winkle, a New York villager of the 1770s who cavorted one night with a ghostly crew of mountain spirits, fell into a deep slumber, and awakened some twenty years later.

Outside the bounds of fiction, the ancient Egyptians labored to retain the appearance, if not the reality, of human life. Preserving the bodies of the dead, they believed, ensured the immortality of the soul. During the third to first millennia BC, Egyptian priests became highly skilled at mummifying the newly dead, employing elaborate dissection and soaking rituals in a process that often took more than two months to complete. Ironically, their procedures included discarding the brain—the organ that Donaldson and other moderns most associate with personal survival. Thousands of years after the embalmers plied their craft, many of the bodies they mummified remain remarkably well preserved—but decidedly dead.

Claims that human beings could also be indefinitely preserved while still alive have surfaced from time to time in India, where yogis in search of enlightenment or celebrity have spent days and even weeks buried alive in underground tombs. Tales of these bizarre burials—which are said to be made possible by a yogi's mastery over mind and body—go back to the 1600s, when ditchdiggers near Amritsar in northwest India uncovered a tomb containing what looked like the mummified body of a young man.

The motionless figure, they later reported, was sitting cross-legged in a dusty chamber, his body draped in faded robes. He appeared quite dead, until the workers carried him out into the sunlight. Then, as the sun's warm rays touched the man's wizened skin, he began to stir. Soon he was able to tell his startled rescuers that he was a fakir, the Indian term for one who works wonders. His name, he said,

was Ramaswami, and he had gone willingly into the tomb almost a century earlier to test his yogic ability.

News of Ramaswami's sensational claim soon spread across India, meeting with almost universal acceptance. The noted Sikh guru Arjun Singh even traveled to meet him and later said he was impressed with the yogi's knowledge of the period in which he claimed to have been born.

The tale of Ramaswami gets a cooler reception from modern authorities, however, in part because there is no record of his original entry into the tomb. Among skeptics, the consensus is that Ramaswami was probably a charlatan who somehow concealed himself in the diggings to capitalize on the popular belief in all-but-unlimited yogic powers.

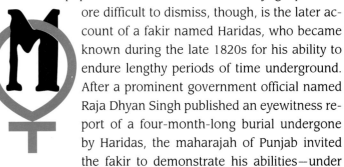

More difficult to dismiss, though, is the later account of a fakir named Haridas, who became known during the late 1820s for his ability to endure lengthy periods of time underground. After a prominent government official named Raja Dhyan Singh published an eyewitness report of a four-month-long burial undergone by Haridas, the maharajah of Punjab invited the fakir to demonstrate his abilities—under controlled conditions at the ruler's own palace in Lahore. Skeptical of Haridas's powers, the maharajah also asked several British doctors and military officers to observe the proceedings for possible fraud.

An 1835 issue of the *Calcutta Medical Times* reported what happened next. To begin with, a preliminary medical examination revealed that Haridas had apparently severed the muscles under his tongue. This enabled him to roll his tongue back and seal the nasal passages at the back of his throat. Haridas's other preparations for his burial were as pragmatic. To empty his digestive tract, he first reduced his diet to milk and yogurt, then he fasted completely. As the great day approached, he performed some of the more extreme cleansing practices of yoga, including swallowing and then regurgitating a strip of linen thirty yards long.

When the moment for his entombment arrived, reported several witnesses, Haridas stuffed wax into his nose

These panels from the coffin of a second-century-BC Egyptian mummy (below) offer a rare depiction of the embalming process—steps that prepare one for the next life. First the body undergoes cleansing (top); then a masked priest leads sacred rituals while the eviscerated body dries in a bed of natron, a form of sodium carbonate (center). Finally, the body, wrapped in linen, wears a painted funeral mask. Beneath the bier are jars containing the mummy's internal organs; only the heart, considered the seat of intelligence, remains in the body.

and ears as protection against insects, positioned himself in the traditional cross-legged pose of a meditating yogi, and retracted his tongue. Almost immediately, his pulse became undetectable. Some of those present then wrapped the motionless Haridas in linen and lifted him into a large chest; according to the memoirs of a British surgeon named McGregor, the chest was then locked, sealed, and placed in "a small apartment below the level of the ground."

Although some air could presumably flow into the "apartment" and the sealed box, the maharajah made arrangements to prevent supplies of food or water from reaching the entranced fakir. As described in McGregor's memoirs, the door of the subterranean room was locked, as was that of the garden house above it; then a wall of bricks and mud was built across the gateway leading to the garden house. Relays of guards watched the new wall around the clock. Forty days later, the maharajah and his guests returned. Making note that the grounds appeared undisturbed, the maharajah ordered the wall torn down, the doors unlocked, and the burial chest opened.

Inside was Haridas, still seated in the same pose as that in which he had been buried. According to McGregor, the fakir manifested every sign of death: His arms and legs were stiff and withered, and his eyes "presented a dim, suffused appearance, like those of a corpse." McGregor could find no pulse in his wrist. Despite these inauspicious symptoms, several attendants gamely set to work on the disinterred yogi, pouring warm water over his head, pulling his tongue forward, removing the wax from his ears and nose, and massaging his stiffened muscles. Using bellows, they pushed air into his lungs. Evidently, the ministrations worked: Within an hour Haridas was completely revived.

McGregor remained certain that the fakir had somehow escaped from the box on the day of the burial, returning just in time for his disinterment; most of those present, however, believed that the safeguards of the locks, the wall, and the guards made any such trick impossible. No longer a skeptic, the maharajah rewarded the fakir with a handful of diamonds. As word of Haridas's spectacular feat spread, worshipful admirers offered him gifts wherever he went.

But his good fortune did not last. Sometime after his performance at the palace, Haridas was accused of sexual improprieties involving several young female followers. His character discredited, he was expelled from Indian high society, never to be heard from again.

Haridas's achievement underground had set a standard that has never been matched. Although live burials by other fakirs have occasionally been reported, few have been as fully documented and none have involved so long a period of time. Many of the allegedly buried yogis have been exposed as frauds. Meanwhile, a number of honest yogis who hoped to emulate Haridas have died trying. The practice of live burials was outlawed in India in 1955, after several holy men expired while attempting the feat. (The burial of living human beings—usually for considerably shorter periods—has also been reported in the West. Harry Houdini, the early-twentieth-century American stage magician, could remain in a submerged, sealed coffin for an hour and a half by slowing his rate of breathing; a French contemporary managed an hour in a coffin of his own.)

Another state closely resembling suspended animation has been recorded around the world by emergency physicians treating those exposed to extreme cold. Acute hypothermia, the medical condition in which core body temperatures drop well below the normal 98.6 degrees Fahrenheit, can stop the heart and lungs, producing a cold, pulseless rigor that emulates death itself. Yet in several celebrated cases, cold victims found unbreathing and without a heartbeat have been restored to life and health.

Nineteen-year-old Jean Hilliard, for example, spent one bitterly cold December night in 1980 lying unconscious in a northern Minnesota farmyard after her car skidded into a nearby ditch. As gusty winds whipped across her body, the air temperature plummeted to fifteen degrees below zero. When the young woman was finally discovered and taken to a local hospital, her body was so rigid that the emergency-room staff could not puncture her skin to administer intravenous fluids. Her temperature had fallen below 88 degrees F. With her heart beating a scant six to eight times a minute and her lungs breathing just three times a minute, doctors could offer little hope of recovery.

Amazingly, however, Hilliard survived. That evening she regained consciousness, and the following afternoon her temperature began to rise. Although she required physical therapy to return circulation to her frostbitten legs and feet, Hilliard experienced no permanent disabilities as a result of her chilling brush with death.

Several children have also been successfully resuscitated after spending twenty to thirty minutes totally submerged in an ice-cold lake or pond. Four-year-old Jimmy Tontlewicz, for example, fell through the frozen surface of Lake Michigan one January day in 1984. By the time rescue divers carried him to shore, the boy had been underwater for at least twenty minutes and appeared clinically dead. His pupils were fixed and dilated, his skin was drained of all color, and neither pulse nor breathing could be detected. Minutes later, when he arrived at a hospital, a special thermometer measured his temperature at just 85 degrees F.

Yet, like Hilliard, the boy responded to medical treatment. An hour after he reached the emergency room, paramedics were able to restore his heartbeat and respiration; within six weeks of his icy plunge, Jimmy was walking, talking, and playing with toys. The experience left its mark, however. After the boy was discharged from the hospital in mid-April, he required extensive speech therapy and began attending a school for children with learning disabilities.

Paradoxically, doctors credited Jimmy's low body temperature with saving his life. His size had helped him to cool quickly; the smaller the body, the faster it loses heat. Because his body was so cold inside, his brain's metabolic rate and its resulting need for oxygen were drastically reduced, greatly extending the length of time he could survive without breathing. Jimmy had probably benefited as well from the "diving reflex," an extreme metabolic resetting that can be triggered by immersion in very cold water. Often stronger in children than in adults, the diving reflex diverts blood from the rest of the body to the heart and brain, the two organs vital to preserving life.

Every winter, public-health officials warn of a more subtle, but sometimes equally deadly, kind of hypothermia that most often afflicts the elderly and the infirm. Because this insidious form of the condition develops gradually, it can go undetected for weeks. Sometimes the root cause is a lack of adequate home heating. But another contributing factor is strictly medical. As people age, they may become less sensitive to chill; even when the temperature inside a dwelling drops to unsafe levels, the occupants may not notice that their bodies have become dangerously cool. Hundreds of cases of walking hypothermia are reported annually in the United States alone; because the disorder is caused in part by a failure in the body's temperature control system, it can be reversed only by externally applied warmth.

For all of hypothermia's dangers, however, a growing number of experts believe that the same condition—if carefully regulated—may actually extend conscious life. The earliest experiments to suggest a connection between low body temperatures

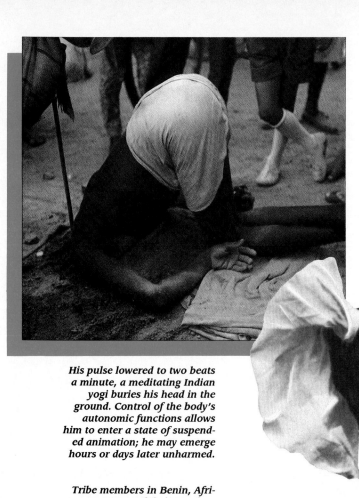

His pulse lowered to two beats a minute, a meditating Indian yogi buries his head in the ground. Control of the body's autonomic functions allows him to enter a state of suspended animation; he may emerge hours or days later unharmed.

Tribe members in Benin, Africa, carry one of their number, drugged and wrapped up, to a temporary burial. The drugs slow bodily functions and induce a trancelike state, during which the participant allegedly taps into magical forces.

and longevity were conducted in 1918 at the Rockefeller Institute for Medical Research—now the Rockefeller University—in New York City by Nobel Prize-winning chemist John Northrop and his colleague Jacques Loeb. In a classic study, Northrop and Loeb demonstrated that fruit flies raised at 50 degrees F. lived nearly nine times longer than those raised at 86 degrees F.

That finding received relatively little attention, perhaps because fruit flies are so biologically different from human beings. Then, some decades later, gerontologist Roy Walford—best known for his interest in therapeutic undernutrition—learned that New England fence lizards live a year longer, on average, than their counterparts in Florida. This brought the phenomenon into the realm of practical information. Lizards, like human beings (and unlike fruit flies), are vertebrates—animals equipped with backbones and roughly similar digestive and circulatory systems. What works for lizards might work for people as well.

To learn more about the relationship between low body temperature and longevity, Walford and colleague Robert Liu decided to study another kind of vertebrate: several species of South American

"annual fish," so called because they live for no more than a year. The fish were so short-lived, the scientists reasoned, that improvements in their longevity would be quickly obvious. Working with specimens Walford had netted in shallow ponds outside Buenos Aires, Walford and Liu produced some remarkable findings in their laboratory at the University of California at Los Angeles.

By keeping the temperature of the tank water, and therefore of the fish, a few degrees colder than the creatures' native ponds, they found they could double the life span of the fish. "Furthermore," Walford reported, "fish reared at 59 degrees F. grew faster and wound up bigger than those reared at 68 degrees F." The "cool" fish were as active as those kept at warmer temperatures, indicating that their metabolic rates probably had not been affected.

Based on the results of that study and others, a number of scientists have speculated that lower body temperature might also have the potential to extend human life. Walford himself has suggested that lowering core temperatures from 98.6 degrees F. to 95 degrees F.—technically, to the point of hypothermia—could increase life expectancy to about 140 years, while re-

mice are stoned but they are not hypothermic."

Another potentially effective drug is an amphetamine-related compound developed by Israeli gerontologists at Bar-Ilan University in Tel Aviv. The medication, they report, can lower the body temperature of animals by as much as five degrees for periods of three to four hours. Unfortunately, the compound is currently too toxic for human use.

Walford has also explored biofeedback as a possible means of lowering body temperature. Biofeedback techniques combine deep relaxation and electronic monitoring equipment to alter such bodily processes as heart rate and blood pressure. When a subject's blood pressure goes above a certain level, for example, a light may glow or a tone may sound. Through repeated practice, the subject learns what mental state will keep the light or sound off by maintaining an acceptably low blood pressure. Changes in body temperature, however, occur much too slowly for biofeedback to be effective. Even after death, Walford points out, the body cools at a rate of only about one degree an hour; in general, physical changes must take place within a minute or two for biofeedback techniques to succeed.

Wondering if there was not some other way that the mind could exert conscious control over body temperature, Walford traveled to India in search of skilled yogic practitioners, masters of the same mental disciplines said to have aided Ramaswami and Haridas in their live burials. One of the many talents attributed to modern yogis is the ability to decrease body temperatures through trance and meditation. After eight months of exhaustive searching, Walford finally found in the caves and forests of the Himalayas an extremely reclusive group of yogis who practiced this very skill. He was astonished to find that most could lower their internal temperatures a full degree at will, while a few seemed to have permanently reduced their core temperatures to between 94 degrees F. and 95 degrees F. Although those val-

searchers at Northwestern University have calculated that the human life span could be increased to 200 years by dropping body temperature a full 7 degrees. Just how to induce a lower internal temperature, however, remains a bit of a puzzle, since humans—unlike fish and fence lizards—are warm-blooded, with internally regulated temperatures that stay fairly constant.

The particular part of the brain that controls body temperature is the hypothalamus, which in humans is located near the base of the skull. This area, which also contributes to the regulation of sleep, hunger, thirst, and the sex drive, constantly monitors internal temperatures, triggering perspiration when the body is too hot and directing muscles to shiver when the body grows too cool. From the viewpoint of longevity researchers trying to reduce their subjects' body temperatures, the hypothalamus is almost too good at its job; it remains stubbornly on guard against any internal temperature change, even a potentially beneficial one. Frustrated scientists have explored several ways to reset this internal thermostat, with little success.

Drugs may offer some promise. In one study, Walford found that tetrahydrocannabinol (THC), the active ingredient of marijuana, could successfully reduce the body temperature of mice—but only temporarily. "I got so excited when it worked, I was going to go on TV and say that grass was the answer to long life," Walford later recalled ruefully. "But then we found that it only works temporarily. The animals become tolerant to the effect and their temperature doesn't go down so far. So after two or three times, the ues fit the medical definition of hypothermia, the men showed no signs of mental or physical lethargy. On the contrary, they appeared active and alert.

Walford returned to the United States believing that human body temperature could indeed be lowered without ill effect. "While becoming a full-time isolated yogic practitioner is hardly feasible for us in the West," Walford wrote in 1982, "my evidence does indicate that successful adaptation to a lower body temperature, if we could find an easier way of lowering it, would be physiologically possible."

Walford himself now believes that the most practical method of lowering body temperature may be caloric restriction—his own preferred method of life extension. Although the mechanisms by which undernutrition affects life span are many, one may be as simple as the fact that animals apparently cool down inside when they eat less food.

Still another strategy for body cooling has been suggested by Angelo Turturro, a staff scientist at the National Center for Toxicological Research in Jefferson, Arkansas. Turturro, who also sees a connection between low body temperature and increased life span, proposed in the late 1980s that bedrooms could be redesigned someday to include cold sleep chambers capable of dropping the human body temperature to between 88 degrees F. and 90 degrees F. Using a microwave generator, such a chamber would mislead the hypothalamus by bathing it in a beam of gentle heat. "The brain would think that the body was 98.6," Turturro told a magazine interviewer in 1988, "but the body would really be cooler."

Turturro acknowledges that his cold sleep chambers would pose some risks. In laboratory experiments, mice in artificial cold torpor have become dependent on the outside environment to control their body temperatures, causing them to freeze to death should heating systems fail. Moreover, Turturro has found that torpor affects the rate at which many cells regenerate—a fact that creates other hazards. When certain intestinal cells fail to reproduce rapidly enough, he points out, the stomach may fall victim to its own digestive acids, producing raging ulcers. Nevertheless,

cold sleep for relatively short periods may be worth the risks, Turturro argues. Spending six hours a night in a cold torpor, he has calculated, could double a sleeper's life span.

Although Turturro's cold sleep chambers strongly suggest the cool, cozy den of a hibernating bear, scientists believe that hypothermia and hibernation are fundamentally different states. One key difference is that a hibernating animal can rouse itself. Human beings in hypothermic coma cannot; unless revived by outside aid, they eventually freeze to death. Moreover, researchers have found that hibernating animals manage their cold dormancy with a range of chemical and behavioral adaptations programmed in at the genetic level. Some animals, for example, automatically put on fat for their winter sleep; others just as instinctively gather food supplies. Many secrete heparin and other anticlotting agents as they hibernate, since blood has a fatal tendency to coagulate when cold. Most important of all, hibernators—unlike hypothermic humans—maintain a stable metabolic balance, so that levels of key blood chemicals remain constant all winter long, rather than dipping within hours. Only by redesigning the human body to perform these and other biochemical feats, researchers conclude, could people safely attempt real hibernation

 nimal hibernation, however, remains an intriguing model for the long-term preservation of dormant human beings. Evidence that hibernating mammals such as woodchucks and ground squirrels live longer than nonhibernating mammals of the same size has given credence to the idea that cold unconsciousness may stop or slow an individual's biological clock, thus extending potential life span. Hibernation may also offer clues to perfecting cryonic suspension. In a phenomenon once considered physiologically impossible, several animal species have been found to freeze solid during the cold winter months.

Since hibernation is a survival strategy for creatures ill adapted to winter, its onset is pegged to the weather; caged

hibernators in warm settings remain active all winter long. In the wild, the onset of cold weather triggers a flurry of activity as animals geared to hibernation seek out safe havens. Dormice scramble into tree holes, snakes slither into communal underground dens, frogs bury themselves in ponds below the frostline, and squirrels settle into leafy nests. Once they are safely hidden, the hibernators enter a state of relative dormancy initiated by a chemical compound known as hibernation-induction trigger, or HIT.

A natural opiate, HIT packs a considerable punch. Even on a balmy summer day, woodchucks and squirrels lapse into a lethargic state when injected with it. More surprising is the effect the same substance has on rhesus monkeys, which do not hibernate in nature. When given HIT, the monkeys sink into a comalike condition in which their hearts beat half as often as usual and their temperatures drop several degrees. Whether HIT could induce a similar state in humans—and whether such a condition could be safely sustained for any length of time—remains unknown.

During natural hibernation, an animal's activities are reduced to a minimum. Heartbeats slow to perhaps a hundredth of the normal rate; breathing and oxygen consumption almost stop. As circulation slows, body temperature drops accordingly. In some animals, the hibernating temperature plummets tens of degrees; in others, such as the bear, it may be only a few degrees lower than normal. (For that reason, some experts consider the bear a deep sleeper rather than a true hibernator.) To an untrained observer, the animals appear to have sunk into a coma. Yet the hibernators typically awaken several times during a single winter, whether to eat from a gathered store of food, to eliminate wastes, or to fend off predators.

In spring, external changes in light and heat, as well as the waning of internal energy reserves, trigger hiber-

Two years after being submerged for an hour in a numbingly cold river, five-year-old Michelle Funk shows no harm from her ordeal. To revive the child—she had no vital signs and a temperature of 66 degrees F.—doctors pumped warmed, oxygenated blood into her. Because extreme cold decreases the brain's oxygen demand, Michelle did not suffer any lasting brain damage.

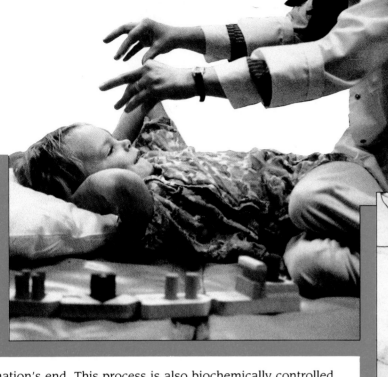

A recuperating Jimmy Tontlewicz (left) touches his ears in response to a physical therapist's question. In 1984, rescue divers pulled him from frigid Lake Michigan (below), where he had fallen through ice while chasing his sled. Although he was underwater for twenty minutes, Jimmy recovered, due in part to the metabolism-slowing effects of hypothermia.

nation's end. This process is also biochemically controlled. As an animal begins to revive, its endocrine system resumes normal activity. This releases enzymes that bring the heart and lungs up to full speed; faster circulation and breathing then warm the body. Within hours, the animal is awake and ready for spring.

Although most hibernating animals become very cool, a number of extraordinary species take hibernation a step further to undergo actual freezing during winter, with much of their body water becoming ice. This bizarre coping behavior is most commonly found among polar insects. One example is the arctic woolly bear caterpillar, which spends up to ten months of the year frozen solid at temperatures as low as −58 degrees F. Investigators have also found that some shellfish, such as mussels and periwinkles, freeze daily in winter when they are exposed at low tide.

The frozen-hibernator phenomenon took on an added dimension in 1982, when William Schmid, a zoology professor at the University of Minnesota, announced that a certain type of frog also froze during winter—the first such case known among amphibians. He reported that the frogs' frozen bodies became so brittle that a leg could snap as easily as a dry tree twig. Intrigued by Schmid's work, Canadian researchers Kenneth Storey and Janet Storey of Carleton University in Ottawa, Ontario, went on to show that several hibernating frog species—the wood frog, the spring peeper, the gray tree frog, and the striped chorus frog—can survive for weeks with as much as 65 percent of their total body water frozen into ice.

Then, in 1988, there came another step up the zoological ladder with the first discovery of a winter-freezing reptile. According to Ronald Brooks of the University of Guelph in southeastern Ontario, young Canadian painted turtles freeze stiff in their nests soon after their birth in late summer. Follow-up studies by the Storeys showed that more than half of the baby turtles' body water turns to ice, making them as rigid as their shells.

While frozen, the insects, shellfish, frogs, and turtles are in a true state of suspended animation. Unlike warmer hibernators, their bodies reveal no movement: Heart, lungs, and all circulation simply stop. Only the brain shows slight neurological activity. Yet when the warm winds of spring arrive, the frozen animals come back to life. For the turtle hatchlings, the great thaw triggers a return of heartbeat and blood flow, followed by breathing. Once defrosted, they emerge eagerly from their nests in search of food. At first, this discovery of freeze-tolerant animals seemed to defy physiological knowledge. If ice forms inside a living cell, the cell quickly ruptures and dies; if too many cells die, so does the animal. When water between the cells freezes, that ice can be equally dangerous, since large crystals can crack cell membranes and sever the connections between cells. Freezing between cells also causes water within the

cells to rush out, dangerously concentrating the salts and other body chemicals that are left behind. If enough fluid leaves the cells, they will crumple and die.

How, then, do turtles, frogs and other animals freeze solid for months without sustaining fatal internal damage? As with ordinary hibernation, adaptations at the molecular level provide the answer—although each freeze-tolerant species has its own slightly different approach to the problem. In most cases, naturally secreted chemicals ensure that the water inside the cells themselves does not freeze, preventing irreparable cellular damage. As for the water between the cells, most animals capable of recovering from freezing produce blood proteins that encourage the slow formation of very small ice crystals instead of membrane-ripping spears of ice. A natural antifreeze known as a cryoprotectant keeps the crystals from growing to dangerous sizes. Some freeze-tolerant animals build up cryoprotectant in the months before hibernation, but others, like the frogs studied by the Storeys, manufacture it in volume only after ice begins to form on their skin.

According to at least one well-known study, animals without natural cryoprotectants may also be able to survive freezing. In a 1954 letter to the scientific journal *Nature*, British researchers Audrey Smith, Alan Parkes, and James Lovelock reported that they had successfully revived golden hamsters after chilling the animals to just below the freezing point. Although some of the animals remained limp, most stiffened, indicating the formation of internal ice. Eventually the frozen hamsters became "wood-like to the touch" and their ears, according to the researchers, "attained the consistency of cardboard."

Not surprisingly, some of the cold, rigid creatures could not be revived. Fifteen of them, however, were successfully brought back to life, making what the letter's authors described as a "complete" recovery. That finding was extraordinary, since it

suggested that mammals—a class that includes humans—could be frozen and then revived. But it remains uncertain, despite the excellent reputation of the three scientists in question, because other researchers have been unable to duplicate the experiment.

Researchers Smith, Parkes, and Lovelock were among the pioneers of the scientific field known as cryobiology, from the Greek *krýos,* or "icy cold." An eminently practical discipline, cryobiology has spawned any number of innovations in medicine, animal husbandry, and zookeeping. Cryobiologists ushered in the era of cryosurgery, in which extreme cold is used to excise warts and reattach retinas; they also contributed to the development of chilling procedures that greatly slow a patient's body functions during delicate brain or heart operations.

The cryobiologists' greatest triumph, however, has been cryopreservation—the artificial storage of living biological materials at temperatures well below freezing, typically by means of chemical cryoprotectants. The process itself is much like that employed for millennia by freeze-tolerant animals; a cryopreservative solution is infused into the specimen to protect cells and limit the scale of ice crystals formed in the spaces between cells. But unlike natural cryopreservation, the artificial technique is not yet perfected. Many cryoprotectants are toxic, and supplying enough of the substance to preserve the cells without poisoning them remains a daunting challenge. Moreover, it is extremely difficult to distribute the cryoprotectant evenly and quickly in larger specimens, such as whole organs.

By the early 1990s, individual cells and simple tissue—from blood cells to bone marrow—had been frozen, preserved, and restored with great success. Even the human embryo had been frozen and stored in liquid nitrogen for days, weeks, or years, then warmed and implanted in a woman's uterus. Because of the limitations of artificial cryopreservation, however, it was not yet technically possible to freeze an organ and make it function later. That tragic limitation meant that an estimated 60 percent of transplantable hearts and 90 percent of transplantable livers deteriorated before they could reach a suitable recipient.

Cryopreservation has long since revolutionized the livestock industry, though. Since the mid-1970s, farmers have used frozen bull semen to interbreed cattle from different continents and to mate living cows with long-dead sires. The technology also plays a vital role in the fight to save endangered animals. In theory, freezing ova and sperm from these creatures may enable preservationists to breed rare animals from different corners of the world or even from different generations, ensuring greater genetic diversity of the species.

In some experimental cases, the frozen embryos of rare animals already have been successfully thawed and implanted in surrogate mothers from related, but unendangered, species. At the Cincinnati Zoo, for example, a common house cat received the thawed egg and sperm of two endangered Indian desert cats in

Frigid water elicits a shocked gasp from a volunteer at the University of Minnesota's Hypothermia Laboratory. The lab studies human beings' response to cold, a subject of interest to gerontologists who see lower body temperatures as a possible avenue to longer lives.

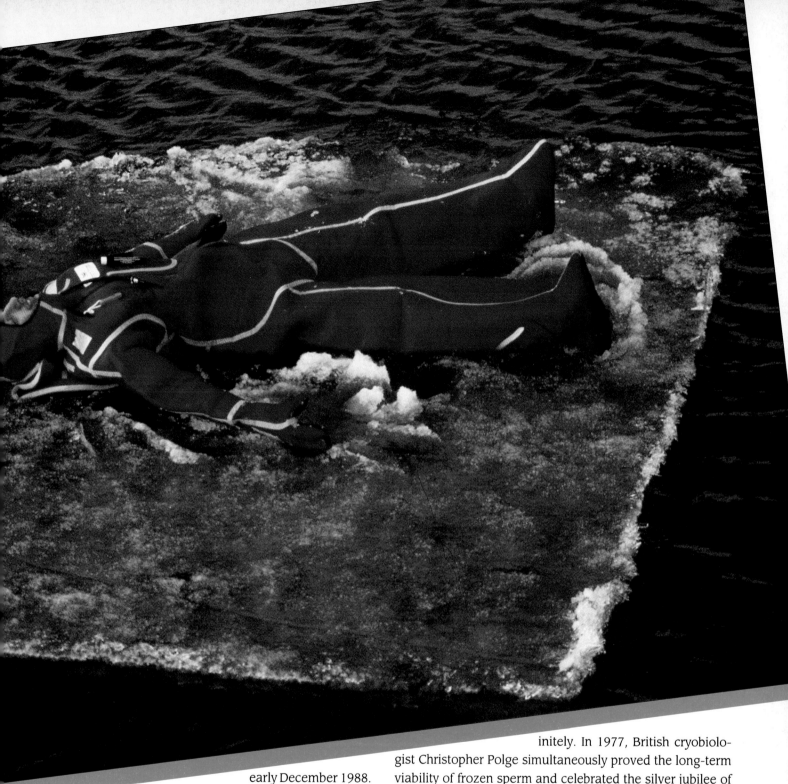

early December 1988.

Nine weeks later, a healthy kitten arrived. The first cat ever born after an interspecies embryo transfer, it was also the first cat born as the result of in vitro fertilization. Such innovative breeding techniques came too late for the dusky seaside sparrow, a species that became extinct in 1987. But when the last of those sparrows died, biologists froze samples of its sperm and bone marrow. They hope to clone new birds one day from the frozen cells.

Indeed, many scientists believe that ova, sperm, and embryos—whether human or animal—can be frozen indef-

initely. In 1977, British cryobiologist Christopher Polge simultaneously proved the long-term viability of frozen sperm and celebrated the silver jubilee of Queen Elizabeth II when he defrosted bull semen collected in 1952, the year of Elizabeth's accession, and used it to inseminate a cow. The thawed sperm "was perfectly healthy and produced a normal calf," Polge revealed to *Omni* magazine in 1981. Queen Elizabeth's reaction, if any, was not recorded.

Polge is not among the futurists who speculate that the long-term freezing of human embryos may one day make it possible to populate far-off solar systems or to ensure the continuation of the human race after a nuclear or

Freezing Human Eggs and Sperm

Bringing frozen bodies back from the dead may seem like science fiction, but for decades medical specialists have been successfully working similar magic on the single human cells from which lives begin. The most advanced work in freezing and reviving living tissue is taking place in the arena of human reproduction.

At more than seventy commercial sperm banks across the United States, fertility specialists freeze the sperm of donors from various ethnic, religious, and educational backgrounds. Although the technology was originally intended to benefit infertile couples, cryonic preservation of the seeds of life also has the potential to confer an indirect kind of immortality. Human sperm and eggs can be frozen and saved for years; in theory, they could be thawed, united, and implanted in surrogate mothers long after the donors were dead.

While artificial insemination has given new hope to those unable to conceive a child by the time-honored method, it can give rise to new problems. One of the most troubling is the chance that sons and daughters of the same donor could unwittingly meet, mate, and produce children together. Perpetuating the genes of a donor in this way could lead not to immortality but to deformities in the offspring of such a union. Recognizing this potential danger, the American Fertility Society recommends the chances of inbreeding be reduced by limiting to ten the number of babies produced from the sperm of a single donor.

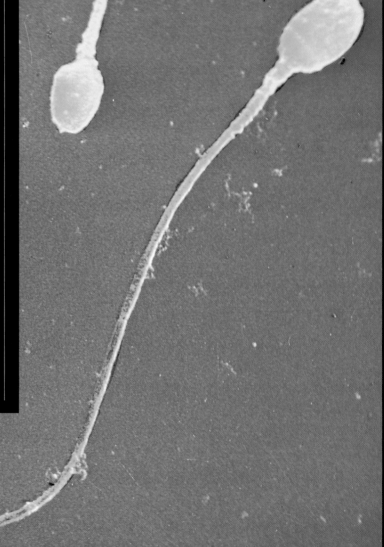

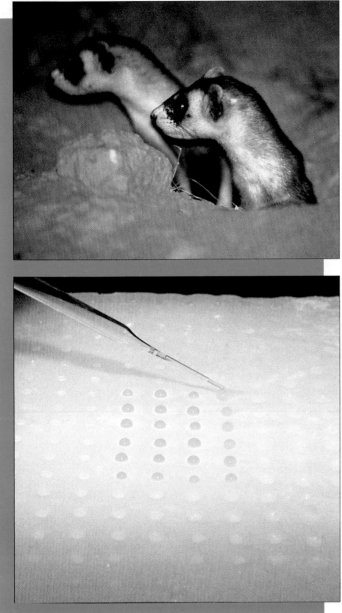

Black-footed ferrets (left), conceived from frozen sperm, are one endangered species that may avoid extinction through artificial insemination. One method of preserving sperm involves dropping semen into holes in a block of ice (below left) to create frozen pellets.

environmental catastrophe, but he sometimes engages in science-fictional ponderings of his own. "Who knows?" he has remarked. "Anthropologists in a thousand years might decide it would be interesting to resuscitate a human being from the present century to see how genetically he would differ from the population of the world in the future."

Although storing a human embryo for birth a millennium hence now appears a practical possibility, scientists remain a long way from the technology that would permit the freezing and later revival of a fully developed human being. The same obstacles that have kept them from freezing whole organs apply with even more force to entire bodies. For cryobiologists, that means there is no medical justification for freezing human beings today in the hope of reviving

them later—a judgment so fundamental to their field that members of the Society for Cryobiology may be expelled for participating in such a procedure. But for cryonics enthusiasts, that logic misses an important point. The technology is here today, they say, to freeze a human body; there is no reason to believe that the technology for reviving such a specimen will not appear in due course.

The crycnicists, who are often enthusiastic amateurs rather than scientists, believe they stand at the threshold of a new and exciting scientific discipline; many compare their field to the infancy of space-rocket science of the 1920s and 1930s, mocked by the scientists of that day but vindicated by the moon flights of the 1960s. Like the early rocket clubs, cryonics is a child of the industrial age. A familiar theme in the science fiction of the 1930s and 1940s, the idea first attracted serious practical interest in 1962.

In that year, a forty-three-year-old physicist named Robert C. W. Ettinger, then a math and physics teacher at a Michigan community college, began circulating the manuscript of a slim but startling book entitled *The Prospect of Immortality*. The book proposed that it was already possible—with 1960s technology—to preserve dead people at very low temperatures until such time as medical science could revive and cure them.

"We need only arrange to have our bodies, after we die, stored in suitable freezers against the time when science may be able to help us," Ettinger wrote. "No matter what kills us, whether old age or disease, and even if freezing techniques are still crude when we die, sooner or later our friends of the future should be equal to the task of reviving and curing us."

In his book, Ettinger stressed how medical definitions of death have changed as resuscitation technologies have advanced. For centuries, he wrote, death was equated with cessation of heartbeat. Modern emergency medicine has made it possible, however, to restart a stopped heart. As a result, death came to be defined by a combination of factors that included the cessation of brain activity.

Ettinger believed that even that definition is too limit-

Sweating for Health

In many cultures, regular sweating is viewed as an important component of a long and healthy life. The *banya*, or "bathhouse," has been a staple of Russian life since the eleventh century; Finnish saunas, such as the one depicted in the 1799 engraving below, are probably even older. In both nations the sweat bath is integrated in rituals for birth, marriage, and even death. In Finland, saunas—including portable ones used by campers—outnumber cars.

The beneficial effects of sweat were recognized as early as 568 BC, when the oldest surviving works on medicine, the Ayurvedic texts, prescribed sweat baths. Modern research shows that sweat, which is 99 percent water, helps regulate body temperature and keep skin clean. It also carries away wastes such as salt, urea, and lactic acid, as well as toxic metals absorbed from polluted air. Some proponents claim that sweating relieves cold symptoms, arthritis, headaches, hangovers, and myriad other ailments.

Early advocates attributed divine powers to sweat baths. The Fox tribe of North America believed that a friendly spirit inside a sweat lodge's heated rocks could extirpate sickness by entering the skin via vapor. Islamic women visited the *hamman*, a Middle Eastern sweat bath, three times before a marriage, with a final rinsing bath on the eve of the wedding. According to Russian and Indian folklore, God created Adam and Eve with drops of falling sweat. Some Hindus also thought that sweat carried the seeds of life: A Bengali tale relates that Shiva wiped his brow with a cloth from which an infant girl was born.

Modern saunas and bathhouses offer more than the cleansing benefits of a simple sweat. At Moscow's famous Sandunov Baths, visitors to the steam room are gently lashed with bundles of birch twigs. The twigs are said to promote circulation and fill the air with a pleasant fragrance.

ing. He described death as a process, not a single moment, and claimed it could be reversed at any point in the process—if only the right technology were available. "Death is not a brick wall or the turning off of a light," he wrote, "but a very complex gradual process which is open to human intervention." From Ettinger's point of view, therefore, freezing a very recently dead body was not much different from freezing a live one. But in practical terms, that distinction made cryonics possible. By waiting until their subjects are pronounced legally dead, cryonicists could avoid charges of murder, manslaughter, or aiding a suicide.

Ettinger first conceived of the idea of cryonic suspension as a teenager in the 1930s. An avid reader of science fiction, the young Ettinger read a story by Neil R. Jones entitled "The Jameson Satellite," in which a professor named Jameson spends millions of years preserved in the frozen reaches of space. He is finally rescued by aliens who revive and repair his brain and then install it in an immortal mechanical body.

"It was instantly obvious to me that the author had missed the main point of his own idea!" Ettinger wrote in *The Prospect of Immortality*, passing over the fact that the Jones story was a piece of fiction. "If immortality is achievable through the ministrations of advanced aliens repairing a frozen human corpse, then why should not everyone be frozen to await later res-

notion of cryonic suspension. They considered cryonics an illegitimate and potentially cultish offspring of cryobiology, replete with concepts that were eccentric at best and fraudulent at worst. Although critics then and since have raised a number of objections to cryonic suspension, the recurrent focus has been on the procedure's single greatest weakness: the cellular damage caused by freezing.

As early as 1969, one skeptic compared the process of freezing a human brain to burning the audiotape of a speech. "Future scientists might be able to reconstruct the tape from its ashes," wrote futurist author Robert W. Prehoda in his book *Suspended Animation,* "but they would have no way of knowing what the original words on the tape might have been. They would simply have a blank tape." Like the words recorded on the burned tape, the complex memory patterns that hold the personality would be lost forever, he argued, when the brain first froze. Other critics do not even envision the recovery of a blank brain. "To believe in cryonics, you would have to believe you could make a cow from hamburger," one prominent cryobiologist has remarked. The British journal *New Scientist* commented still more tellingly in 1988, "Anyone who has tasted a defrosted raspberry can testify to the dire, irreversible effects of ice on biological material."

Ettinger himself believes that not even the most eminent scientist can predict what is to come; he contends that cryonicists are simply more optimistic about the future of

cue by our own people?"

A decade later, during a hospital stay brought on by earlier war injuries, Ettinger heard about the fledgling science of cryobiology and its experiments with frozen tissue. After the war, he continued his interest in cryobiology, reading everything he could on the topic. The more he read about how cells could be frozen, rewarmed, and brought back to life, the more he believed the same could be done with entire human beings. Eventually, he decided to write a book and present his ideas to the world.

With the publication of *The Prospect of Immortality,* which has been reprinted several times in at least four languages, Ettinger became something of a minor celebrity. Several small but fervent cryonics organizations sprang into existence, with members signing up to have their bodies frozen after death in the hope that future medical technology could "reanimate" them. As suggested in Ettinger's book, applicants planned to pay for the procedure by means of life-insurance policies, with a cryonics facility listed as the beneficiary.

Most scientists, however, strongly resisted the entire

medical science than are the skeptics. As for the wave of criticism, he suggests that his own modest credentials may have worked against the movement's credibility. "I knew I carried no weight, had no formal qualifications, and was not suited for a leadership role," he wrote in 1987. "But as the years passed and no one better came forward, I finally had to write."

Despite its critics, cryonics has continued to attract a small but steady stream of self-described "immortalists," who estimate their own numbers at about 600 worldwide. Most are white men in their thirties or forties, interested in science fiction, usually atheistic or agnostic, and with a technical background, often in computer science. Many of them learned about the movement through Ettinger's book.

One of the more prominent immortalists is Arthur Quaife, who came upon Ettinger's book in the 1960s while a graduate student in mathematical logic at the University of California at Berkeley. He was instantly drawn to its message. "Here was just what I'd been considering," he later recalled, "wondering to what extent medical science might progress in my lifetime so I would never have to die."

uaife met with Ettinger in Michigan and upon returning to California joined one of the first cryonics organizations, now called the American Cryonics Society, or ACS. In the ensuing years, he became the president and driving force of Trans Time, Inc., the facility that performs freezing operations for ACS members. Working eighty-hour weeks, Quaife appeared to one reporter to be "spending over two-thirds of his waking life preparing for the next one," a characterization with which Quaife agreed. Trans Time, which is operated for profit, is one of three American organizations actively engaged in cryonic suspension. The others are the Cryonics Institute in Oak Park, Michigan, which Ettinger helped found, and the Alcor Life Extension Foundation in Riverside, California. Alcor, which has never been a stranger to publicity, is the organization that cancer patient Thomas Donaldson selected to freeze and store his head.

As practiced by all three organizations, the preservation process itself is fairly straightforward. Ideally, it begins almost immediately after a person is pronounced legally dead—before the destructive processes unleashed by death have advanced too far. First, the body is put on a heart-lung resuscitator to supply oxygen to the cells. Various stabilizing drugs are administered to minimize damage to the brain and to maintain the body's overall physiological condition. Then the body is cooled and brought to a storage facility, where it is packed in dry ice. Cryonicists then remove the blood and replace it with a cryoprotective blood substitute—a glycerol "antifreeze" solution intended to limit the damage from the formation of internal ice crystals.

Once the body registers a temperature below the freezing point, it is placed in a torpedo-shaped stainless-steel "cryocapsule" filled with liquid nitrogen. There it will be maintained at a frigid -321 degrees F., a temperature at which, according to cryonicists, "biological processes"—presumably meaning decay—"that require one second at normal body temperature take more than thirty trillion years." The entire suspension process, from death to cryocapsule, can take days or weeks, depending on the circumstances and the subject's physiology.

Such is the ideal scenario. In real life, cryonicists have not always been notified immediately after death has occurred; on occasion, they have had to apply their arts several hours, or even a few days, after the fatal moment. Even the most devoted cryonics enthusiasts doubt the efficacy of treatment in such cases—but since cold storage can do no more harm, and might conceivably still work, the technique is often applied anyway.

Two methods of suspension are available. Some people opt for the traditional, and perhaps more psychologically appealing, whole body suspension; others, such as Thomas Donaldson, prefer to preserve only their heads, a process known as neurosuspension. Those who choose to freeze only their heads are betting that brain transplants will be routine one day, perhaps even easier to perform than the revival of a body enfeebled by disease or old age.

founder of the cryonics movement, poses before a two-body cryocapsule at his Cryonics Institute in Oak Park, Michigan. Established in 1976, the institute has taken on only four "patients," including Ettinger's mother, Rhea (right), who he claims "may be the first of our generation to achieve immortality through the skills of future medicine." Ettinger does not guarantee resurrection, but his brochure observes, "From a medical standpoint, you have nothing to lose. You are already clinically and legally dead when you are frozen, and at worst you will simply remain dead."

Or, in a still more sophisticated scenario, no transplant may be necessary at all; instead the new body might be grown right around the old brain. "You're talking about a technology that can pretty much have complete control over living systems," says Alcor cryonicist Mike Darwin. "It may actually be more of a tour de force to repair a whole-body patient than to repair a neuro patient." In most cases, neurosuspension costs less as well—$41,000 to $75,000, depending on the facility, compared with as much as $140,000 for a whole body suspension.

Neurosuspension has also given cryonicists a rare glimpse into the results of their endeavors. On occasion, subjects in whole body suspension have been "converted" to neurosuspension when their funds be-

Cryonics entrepreneur Arthur Quaife advises prospective clients, including those shown with him in the top picture, to pay for freezing through life-insurance coverage: "Fifty cents a day for immortality. I like the deal."

gan to run low. Alcor's Mike Darwin has conducted autopsies on the resulting headless bodies, with what might seem to be discouraging results. Although he saw no signs of decay, he reported that major organs such as the lungs and heart were split down the middle as a consequence of the cold. Those findings left Darwin still confident in the cryonics process. "Given this, you might say these guys are lunatics to be freezing someone, but these fractures hardly disturb me," he told one reporter. "We knew we'd have to go in and make repairs."

The first known cryonic suspension occurred in 1967, when a former California psychology professor named James Bedford was declared dead of a longstanding case of lung cancer by his personal physician.

Bedford was quickly frozen by a team of cryonics enthusiasts, including Robert Nelson, a one-time prizefighter and owner of a television repair shop. Although Bedford himself had arranged for the suspension and had also left money for further cryonics research, his suspension resulted in the first of many legal controversies that have dogged the cryonics movement.

Outraged that family money was being diverted to keep their grandfather's body in liquid nitrogen, several of the Bedford grandchildren sued to have the will overturned and the suspension terminated. In the end, legal costs consumed much of the estate, the additional cryonics research was ended, and Bedford remained on ice. The publicity that surrounded the case was also a source of angry disputation; Bedford himself, according to some participants, had desired total anonymity, yet at least one of the cryonics enthusiasts had named him to the press. Details of Bedford's suspension were also revealed in Robert Nelson's 1968 book, *I Froze the First Man.*

Since the Bedford suspension, between two dozen and three dozen more suspensions have occurred. A few months after Bedford was frozen, for instance, the body of Steven Mandell, a college student who had died (or, as cryonicists prefer to say, became "deanimated") from an abdominal infection, was also placed in liquid nitrogen. Others soon followed, including those of the wife of a New York policeman and the parents of a midwestern judge.

One of the first neurosuspensions involved the brain of fifteen-year-old Patricia "Luna" Wilson, daughter of science fiction author Robert Anton Wilson. The teenager was bludgeoned to death in 1968 by a deranged man while she was closing up a clothing store for a friend in Berkeley, California. Her body lay undiscovered until the following day.

The Wilson family decided to have Luna put in cryonic suspension. For help, they turned to physiologist Paul Segall, a researcher with interests in both cryonics research and cloning. A longtime friend of the family who had recently begun working with Arthur Quaife at Trans Time, Segall took immediate action. State law required an autopsy of all homicide victims, so that in this instance a total body suspension made little sense. Only the brain, which had been removed and studied as part of the examination, could be preserved. Fortunately, the body had been refrigerated after its discovery. Segall rushed to the medical examiner's office with a container filled with dry ice. Luna's brain was placed in the container and then taken to Trans Time's facilities and immersed in a liquid nitrogen cryocapsule— where it has remained ever since.

Given the time lapse between the murder and her cryonic immersion, Luna Wilson must remain one of the less likely candidates for a successful revival. "We feel it is a long shot," her father later commented. "But it's our way of expressing our belief in life and our rejection of the casual acceptance of murder and death in our society." For him, as for the relatives of several other cryonics "patients," the procedure seemed as much a symbolic defiance of death as a real hope for future life.

The ethics of charging tens of thousands of dollars for such consolation sometimes troubles cryonics conservators. "This case certainly gives me pause," Alcor's Mike Darwin has said of a young Spanish woman whose body was autopsied before she was shipped in dry ice to Los Angeles for a whole body suspension. "Everyone, even her family, understands her chances are infinitesimal." Although Alcor tried to dissuade her relatives from going ahead with the procedure, Darwin says, her family, like the Wilsons, stood firm. And so, in Darwin's words, the woman remains in suspension as someone "who desperately needs to be cared for and protected, toward a time when medicine is equal to her needs."

One of the cryonics industry's more chilling stories— involving a facility that, in the end, proved not quite chilling enough—centered around Cryonics Interment, a firm based in Chatsworth, California, and run by the same Robert Nelson who had helped to freeze James Bedford. The company, whose staff consisted primarily of Nelson himself, failed in

As president of Alcor Life Extension Foundation, Carlos Mondragon, seen here with a cryocapsule at his California headquarters, has been at the center of several legal clashes, among them a standoff with authorities who are unhappy about bodies—frozen or not—being stored in a warehouse.

May 1979 when, according to Nelson, he could no longer pay the liquid-nitrogen bills. Strapped for cash, he allowed the nine frozen bodies in his care to thaw and decompose.

"When we saw the cryotorium we found it to be filthy, full of stench and neglected," said one man who had made a $15,000 down payment to freeze his mother and father. He and relatives of several of Nelson's other deceased customers sued Nelson for breach of contract and fraud. Although Nelson argued in court that cryonics was a high-risk business and that he had made no guarantees, the jury awarded the relatives more than $900,000. The moral verdict of many cryonicists was still more severe. Most saw Nelson as no better than a Hitler—a comparison made by at least one author—since by cryonics standards his decision to thaw the bodies was an act of mass murder.

A decade later, Nelson gave his version of the now-notorious Chatsworth incident to a cryonics newsletter, the *Venturist Monthly News.* The interview, approved by Nelson himself, painted a telling portrait of a man in over his head. In his zeal for the cryonic cause, said Nelson, he had frozen the bodies of people whose estates and relatives contributed little or no money for maintenance. Borrowing funds from wealthy "patients" to maintain poor ones, Nelson had resorted to storing two or three bodies inside cryocapsules originally intended for one, stashing the liquid-nitrogen-filled cylinders in vaults at nearby cemeteries.

Then, according to Nelson, an unreported power failure stopped a pump that had been supplying liquid nitrogen to a leaky cryocapsule containing an older woman and an eight-year-old girl who had died of cancer. Without the constant addition of coolant, the faulty capsule gradually returned to the temperature of its surroundings. For Nelson, the discovery of the failed pump was the last straw. "The capsule is *warm!* WARM!" he recollected. "I fell to the ground and I cried. God, that little girl—" Nelson refroze the corpses without examining them, but he had clearly lost faith in their ultimate viability. By 1979, he ran out of money

and let all nine of the bodies go. "I was able to say 'I did my best,' " he told the *Venturist Monthly News.* "I promised to freeze them, which I did. I didn't promise to pay the bill for eternity, which no one would or could expect."

If the Chatsworth incident publicized the worst side of the cryonics business, a flurry of news stories in 1987 portrayed the movement in a more positive, and even scientifically respectable, light. In April of that year, Paul Segall, by now an officer of Trans Time and a visiting scholar in anatomy and physiology at the University of California at Berkeley, announced the results of an experiment in which a frisky three-year-old beagle spent fifteen minutes in a near-frozen, deathlike state—and lived to bark about it later.

Inspired by Smith, Parkes, and Lovelock's early cryobiological experiments with freezing golden hamsters, Segall and his University of California colleagues had been conducting similar research for some time at a laboratory on the university's Davis campus. Their goal was to keep hamsters and dogs alive at low temperatures by replacing the animals' blood with artificial cryoprotectants, a technique Segall refers to as chilled bloodless perfusion. The beagle experiment was their best success story to date.

As Segall's press release described the procedure, the beagle had been anesthetized, then immersed in a tub of ice-water slush. Soon his temperature plummeted from about 101 degrees F. to below 70 degrees F. As the dog's heart stopped beating, the experimenters attached a canine heart-lung machine with which they gradually drained his blood, replacing it with a cooled substitute containing large amounts of glycerol. Meanwhile, the dog's temperature continued to fall. By the time it reached 38 degrees F.—just 6 degrees above the freezing point—all signs of life had vanished and the beagle appeared clinically dead.

At that point, the scientists turned off the heart-lung machine, keeping the dog in his deathlike state for fifteen minutes. Then the revival began. With the machine again functioning, the experimenters bathed the beagle's body in warm water as they returned the blood to his veins. When the dog's internal temperature reached 80 degrees F., the electric paddles of a defibrillator were applied to his chest to bring back his own heartbeat. Soon the dog's lungs inflated and he began breathing on his own. From that moment, said the experimenters, recovery was quick and complete.

"Within a few days, he was up and about," Segall reported. "The wounds from the incisions had to heal, but apart from that he was fine." An exuberant Segall adopted the beagle as his own pet, naming him Miles after the Woody Allen character in the 1973 film *Sleeper* who awakens from cryonic suspension two centuries after undergoing a failed appendectomy. Six months after the experiment, Segall and Miles made appearances on nationally syndicated television talk shows.

As a Trans Time officer and an applicant for suspension, Segall has linked chilled bloodless perfusion to future developments in cryonics technology. He is quick to point out, however, that the same technique could have other, more mainstream, medical uses. Bloodless surgery could make operations that involve a great deal of blood loss, such as coronary bypass, much safer. "Bleeding is the biggest cause of death in surgery," neurosurgeon Julian Bailes, who practices low-temperature surgery at Pittsburgh's Allegheny General Hospital, commented in Segall's 1989 book *Living Longer, Growing Younger.* "If you could put someone in a state of suspended animation, you could operate in a totally bloodless field." In addition, he observes, because such operations would require little or no blood transfusion, the risk of infection from contaminated donor blood would be greatly reduced.

Segall has also suggested that one day blood substitutes could be used in multiorgan transplant operations, both to keep the donated organs viable and to keep prospective recipients alive until suitable organs became available. In a still more imaginative application, he envisions a sophisticated subzero form of the same procedure being used for short-term cryonic suspensions. Astronauts, for instance, could be placed in suspended animation aboard their spacecraft if they became injured or seriously ill, giving them time to return to earth for treatment. Back on earth,

according to Segall, patients suffering from such modern scourges as AIDS, cancer, or Alzheimer's disease could be frozen for several months, revived for a few days or weeks, and then frozen again. Such cycles of freezing and thawing might help patients slow the progression of their illnesses— and thus postpone their deaths—until a cure is found.

Despite those intriguing possibilities, however, Segall's beagle study itself does not mean that the revival of cryonically suspended human beings is imminent. Unlike cryonic subjects, Miles never dropped below the freezing point—much less to the −321 degrees F. level of liquid nitrogen storage. Nor, critics say, was his chilling experience particularly groundbreaking. Similar, if not quite so cold, canine experiments were performed by navy scientists in the 1960s. And officials at the Alcor cryonics facility have huffily stated that their organization has kept cryoprotected dogs alive at 39.2 degrees F. for four hours at a time; they simply did not publicize it.

Several months after the beagle announcement, Alcor had its own share of publicity—this time, mostly negative. The story involved a landmark legal case that began in December 1987, when Saul Kent, a longtime member of the cryonics movement, transferred his dying eighty-three-year-old mother, Dora, to the Alcor facility. By housing her on the premises, Kent hoped that the suspension process could start as soon as possible after she passed away. As expected, his mother soon died. Approximately eight hours after her heart stopped beating, according to Kent, the technicians at Alcor injected stabilizing drugs, replaced her blood with a cryoprotectant, began cooling her body, and removed her head for permanent storage.

All of this activity followed standard cryonic procedure, with one exception: No doctor had been present to certify the cause of Dora Kent's death, as required by state law. After first declaring that Dora had died of pneumonia, a county coroner changed his mind and announced that Dora might have died from a dose of barbiturates administered at

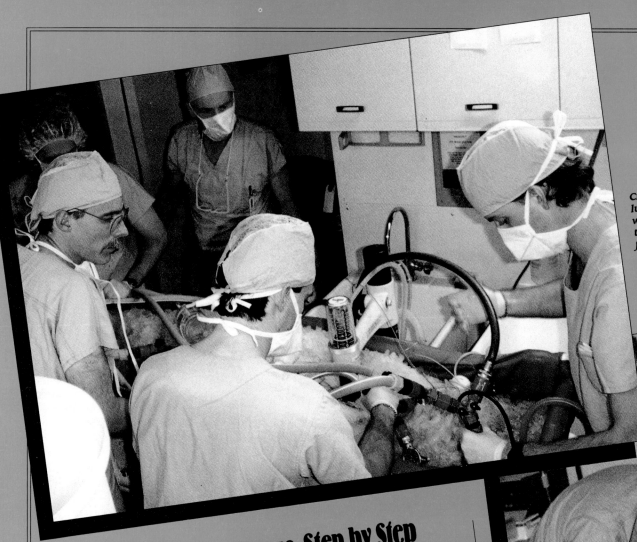

Cryonicists adjust a heart-lung resuscitator (left), which is used to replace the body's blood and tissue fluids with a glycerol-based antifreeze that minimizes ice damage to cells.

Technicians swathe the body in plastic bags (above) before its immersion in the cooling bath. The body is chilled about 6 degrees F. an hour until it reaches –110 degrees F.

Into the Deep Freeze, Step by Step

Cryonic suspension is a complicated process, which for best effect, cryonicists claim, should commence within minutes of the "patient's deanimation." (Enthusiasts are careful to use these terms to reflect their belief that death is not permanent.) When a prospective patient dies, a cryonics team is dispatched to pick up the body. Once death has been officially declared—and if no autopsy is required—the technicians feed intravenous medications into the subject's bloodstream to stabilize cell membranes, inhibit blood clotting, and protect the digestive system against its own acids. The body is packed in ice to begin reducing its core temperature, while a heart-lung resuscitator keeps blood circulating. The patient is ready for transport to the cryonics laboratory.

There, the body is prepared for surgery. A hole is drilled through the skull to monitor brain swelling, which can occur during freezing. The blood is replaced with a solution containing glycerol, a polyalcohol related to that used in antifreeze; this so-called perfusate is intended to minimize cell damage from the freezing process.

Next, the body is placed in a bath of silicone oil, which is gradually chilled to –110 degrees F. Then the patient is zipped inside two heavy-duty sleeping bags and placed in a cryocapsule (a stainless-steel vacuum bottle) for further cooling. Finally, the body is transferred to a second cryocapsule, big enough for four patients, and stored head-down, so that if the liquid nitrogen level ever falls, the brain will be the last body part to thaw.

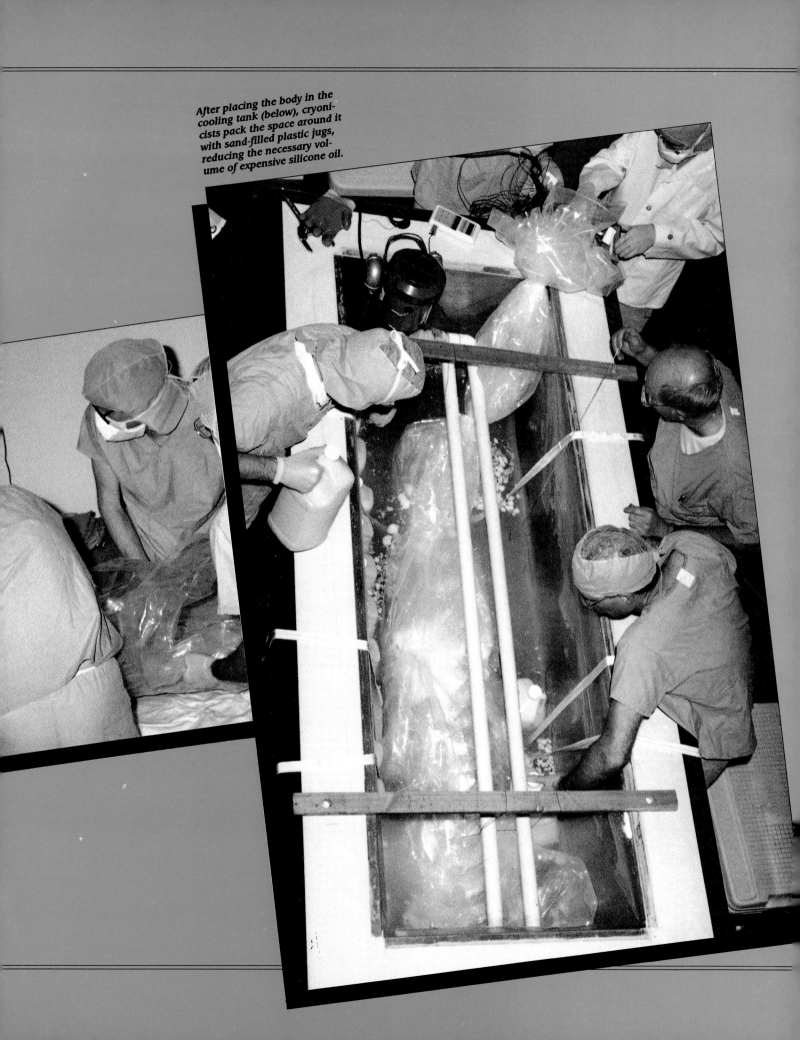

After placing the body in the cooling tank (below), cryonicists pack the space around it with sand-filled plastic jugs, reducing the necessary volume of expensive silicone oil.

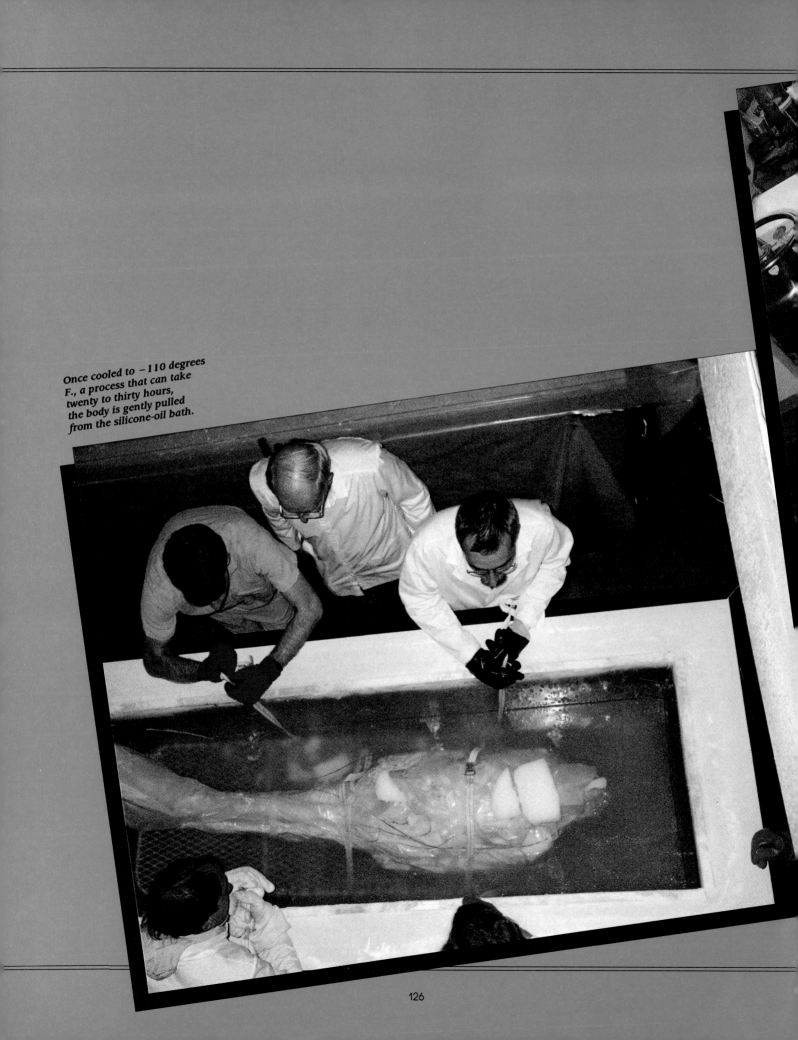

Once cooled to − 110 degrees F., a process that can take twenty to thirty hours, the body is gently pulled from the silicone-oil bath.

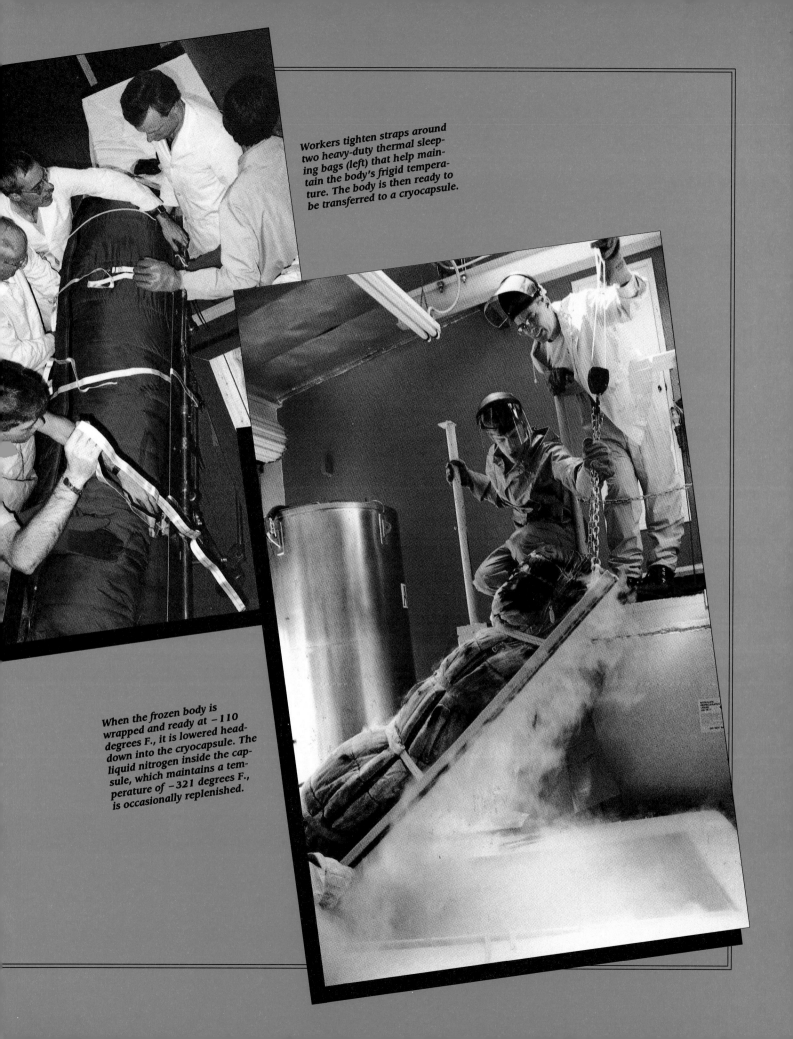

Workers tighten straps around two heavy-duty thermal sleeping bags (left) that help maintain the body's frigid temperature. The body is then ready to be transferred to a cryocapsule.

When the frozen body is wrapped and ready at −110 degrees F., it is lowered head-down into the cryocapsule. The liquid nitrogen inside the capsule, which maintains a temperature of −321 degrees F., is occasionally replenished.

Alcor. Alcor retorted that the barbiturates were part of a standard injection given after death to aid the freezing process. Yet the coroner's accusation left the macabre suggestion that Dora Kent had prematurely lost her head.

Although Kent insisted his mother had been legally dead before the suspension process began, the coroner maintained that a proper postmortem was required to determine just what had happened. An autopsy, however, would have required defrosting the head—an unthinkable action for the cryonicists. So they took Dora's head into hiding, where it remained during the ensuing legal battle. In the hectic months that followed, Alcor equipment was confiscated, then returned, and several Alcor staff members were arrested, then released without being charged. Eventually, all charges against the facility were dropped, and Dora Kent's head remained frozen. In the meantime, Alcor adopted new guidelines that included notifying the coroner of all impending suspensions before they took place.

Since their work began in the 1960s, cryonics enthusiasts have become accustomed to criticism. Many skeptics view them as naive dreamers with an unrealistic faith in science. Others see them as moral cowards who refuse to face the inevitability of death. Undeniably, their approach to life and death has created an incredible thicket of legal and ethical issues. By the 1990s, candidates for suspension confronted a stack of forms weighing four and a half pounds, intended to cover every legal, financial, and medical contingency related to the process. Yet despite the many complications and the disdain of others, cryonicists are unshakably certain that someday their frozen patients will revive and live again to thank them for their pioneering sacrifices.

"Clearly, the freezer is more attractive than the grave, even if one has doubts about the future capabilities of science," wrote Robert Ettinger in 1962. "With bad luck, the frozen people will simply remain dead, as they would have in the grave. But with good luck, the manifest destiny of science will be realized, and the resuscitees will drink the wine of centuries unborn."

For that happy scenario to unfold, however, medical technology must overcome some truly daunting obstacles. Aside from the matter of perfecting human cloning to produce replacement bodies, the thawing process itself remains beyond present-day capabilities. Bringing back cells from low temperatures is an extremely difficult process because the ice crystals that damage cells and tissue form during thawing as well as during cooling. Scientists have also found that different types of cells may need to be thawed at different rates.

For many in the cryonics movement, an encouraging sign that help is on the way came in 1986 with the publication of K. Eric Drexler's book *Engines of Creation*. Drexler, a computer scientist who trained at the Massachusetts Institute of Technology, has since served as a research affiliate at MIT's Artificial Intelligence Laboratory and a visiting scholar at Stanford University. In his book, he coined the term *nanotechnology* to describe a future generation of molecule-size machines so small that they would be measured in nanometers—tens of billionths of an inch.

Inspired by the tiny living mechanisms of the cell, Drexler's nanomachines could be designed for a universe of applications. Some of the devices he proposed would build skyscrapers or spaceships far more quickly than microscopic corals build reefs; others of a medical bent might be designed to cruise the body's circulatory system, destroying any fat cells they encountered. Ultimately, according to Drexler, nanotechnology could also be designed to reverse the cellular damage caused by freezing and thawing. In his analysis of cryonic suspension, Drexler argued that the first step, freezing, is well within modern capabilities through the use of chemical fixatives and artificial cryoprotectants. In his view, the crucial second step, thawing, can be safely left to the nanoengineers of the future, since even extensive cell damage could be repaired if the basic arrangement of cells remained.

Once the engineers develop the nanomachines capable of reversing cryonic suspension, scientists would tackle

Miles, the beagle that was clinically dead for fifteen minutes in a near-freezing experiment at the University of California, watches physiologist Paul Segall at work. Now that a dog has survived the process, said Segall's collaborator and fellow physiologist Hal Sternberg, "we'll go to monkeys."

the easiest cases first—those patients frozen most recently, by relatively sophisticated methods. Working backward, the life restorers would then turn to subjects frozen by earlier and cruder techniques. Finally, the doctors would attempt to revive a cryonically suspended patient of today—in Drexler's scenario, a heart-attack victim.

"In the first stage of preparation, the patient lies in a tank of liquid nitrogen," Drexler wrote of the surgical recovery that nanotechnology might make possible. "Surgical devices designed for use at low temperatures reach through the liquid nitrogen to the patient's heart. There they remove solid plugs of tissue to open access to major arteries and veins. An army of nanomachines equipped for removing protectant moves through these openings, clearing first the major blood vessels and then the capillaries."

After the first nanomachines open up the circulatory system, the physicians in Drexler's futuristic scenario would "pump in a milky fluid containing trillions of devices that enter cells and remove the glassy protectant, molecule by molecule." Like miniature maintenance workers, the machines replace the protectant "with a temporary molecular scaffolding that leaves ample room for repair machines to work." When the nanomachines encounter such obstacles as molecules that must be moved aside, Drexler continues, "the machines label them for proper replacement."

With the protectant eliminated, the patient would be warmed to just above freezing. Tiny cell-repair machines would enter the cells through the blood vessels, while other minuscule devices would repair the damaged heart and weakened arteries. To avoid "premature, unbalanced activity," however, most of each cell's active molecules would remain "blocked"—incapable of chemical interaction.

As revival approached, the medical pace would quicken. "Outside the body, the repair system has grown fresh blood from the patient's own cells. It now transfuses this blood to refill the circulatory system," Drexler explains. "Metabolism resumes step by step; the heart muscle is finally unblocked on the verge of contraction. Heartbeat resumes, and the patient emerges into a state of anesthesia."

And, to ensure that the patient revives not only healthy but without postoperative scarring, other nanomachines sew the skin and underlying tissues seamlessly together. Finally, to conclude the imaginative scenario, "the remaining devices in the cells disassemble one another into harmless waste or nutrient molecules. At last, the sleeper wakes refreshed to the light of a new day."

Conventional scientists remain ambivalent about Drexler's visions of the future. Drexler himself agrees with critics who foresee the possibility of a runaway horde of badly programmed nanomachines, capable of inadvertently destroying the planet as they proceed on a misguided mission of disassembly and reconstruction. More fundamentally, some physicists have asked whether machines so small might not be irreparably damaged by the constant motion that is characteristic of all molecules or by the background radiation that pervades all space.

The cryonicists, however, are definitely impressed. "The biological repair potential of cell repair technology appears so vast," wrote one enthusiast in 1988, "it might just be simplest to ask whether there is anything this technology *couldn't* fix." Still more telling has been the commercial reaction. After the publication of Drexler's book, engineers "began applying by the six-pack" for cryonic suspension, according to Alcor president Carlos Mondragon.

Indeed, as the horizons of modern technology expand, the notion of suspended animation, like that of extending conscious life, becomes ever less fantastic. Whether by dreaming away the decades in a cryocapsule, or by living longer and healthier lives through techniques as yet unproven or even undreamed of, future generations may take encounters with their own great-great-grandchildren as a matter of course. "Grow old along with me," wrote nineteenth-century poet Robert Browning. "The best is yet to be: the last of life, for which the first was made." Browning himself died in 1889 at age seventy-seven—exceeding the accepted life expectancy of a male by thirty years. Little more than a century after his death, techniques may be emerging to fulfill the promise of his timeless words.

Water's Timeless Power

From the beginning of time, water has been linked to the mysteries of human existence. In folk tales and legends, it is a magic fluid that gives life, cures diseases, and bestows youth, wisdom, and immortality. Many early civilizations developed water cults, believing that the sounds and movements of running streams signaled the presence of a living spirit.

Later societies—including the Greeks, Romans, and Japanese—placed a high value on the restorative properties of water. The Romans, in particular, treasured the seemingly miraculous powers of naturally occurring hot springs and mineral-enriched waters. Daily bathing, they believed, could literally wash away such afflictions as leprosy, tumors, infertility, and melancholia. In time, an elaborate tradition of public bathing emerged, designed to promote health, ensure long life, and enhance physical beauty.

As the Roman Empire spread, so too did public bathing. Today, in the German city of Baden-Baden, the tradition continues on the site where a Roman bath once stood. In ancient times, the complex boasted a grand Emperor's bath, an equally splendid chamber for his soldiers, and a third pool for their horses. Horses are no longer welcome, but more than 600,000 humans flock to the public pools at Baden-Baden each year to immerse themselves in an ancient tradition. Many are seeking relief from a host of ills—although physicians disagree as to the therapeutic benefits of the water treatments—while others are simply taking the opportunity to relax and rejuvenate in the warm, soothing waters.

Its mild climate ensured by the Black Forest mountains that shelter it on three sides, the German city of Baden-Baden provides an idyllic setting for its famous hot springs baths.

Spouting the mineral-rich water from more than a mile underground, a bronze statue at Baden-Baden recalls an ancient belief that springs are sources of youth and rejuvenation.

Hot Baths That Entrance the World

From Roman times on, the baths at Baden-Baden have attracted Europe's most celebrated figures. Emperor Frederick III was so revitalized after a visit in 1473 that he later declared the town his royal seat. During the 1800s, German composer Johannes Brahms and Russian novelist Fyodor Dostoyevsky visited the hot springs. And American humorist Mark Twain became an enthusiastic convert during a two-week stay in 1879. "I fully believe I left my rheumatism in Baden Baden," he wrote in his journal. "Baden Baden is welcome to it."

Today, visitors are drawn to two bathhouses, the Renaissance-style Friedrichsbad, completed in 1878, and the modern Caracalla Therme, opened in 1985. As in ancient times, water registering 160 degrees F. is drawn from sources located deep below ground and pumped to the baths. There it is cooled to between 85 and 100 degrees F. and used in bathing treatments, moist-heat saunas, and inhalation therapies. Also, many visitors report benefits from drinking the sulfur-rich water, although it is said to have an unpleasant briny taste.

A pair of bathers bask in a dry-heat sauna as part of a fifteen-stage treatment at the Friedrichsbad spa. The process, known as a Roman-Irish bath, also includes a soap-and-brush massage and full immersion in the mineral-rich spring water.

Beneath the ornate rotunda of one of the Friedrichsbad's baths, visitors soak in a thermal pool. As part of a procedure thought to stimulate the metabolism and improve circulation, bathers move through a series of pools that progressively become warmer, then colder.

Blending elements of classical and modern architecture, the spa at Caracalla Therme features hot-springs-fed swimming pools, baths, waterfalls, water spouts, and fountains. The complex is named for Roman Emperor Marcus Aurelius Antoninus—also known as Caracalla—who laid the cornerstone for the first baths at Baden-Baden in the third century AD.

The hot spray from a mushroom-shaped fountain massages a bather's neck and shoulders. The soothing water is said to have preventive as well as recuperative powers for those who are affected by the stress of everyday life.

ACKNOWLEDGMENTS

The editors would like to thank the following for their assistance: Arne Bey, Life Services Supplements, Inc., Atlantic Highlands, New Jersey; Nicolette Bromberg, University of Kansas Libraries, Lawrence; Professor Helmut Jung, Istituto Archeologico Germanico, Rome; Helene Kronimus, Bäder-und Kurverwaltung, Baden-Baden, Germany; Sandra Martin, Paraview, New York; Gabrielle Riehle, Bäder-und Kurverwaltung, Baden-Baden, Germany; Christine Vary, Bäder-und Kurverwaltung, Baden-Baden, Germany.

PICTURE CREDITS

BIBLIOGRAPHY

Academic American Encyclopedia. Princeton, N.J.: Aretê, 1980.

Allardice, Pamela, *Aphrodisiacs and Love Magic.* Bridport, England: Prism Press, 1989.

Anderegg, Karen, "A Spa Idyll." *Vogue,* December 1984.

Angier, Natalie:
"Animal Studies Link Low Calories to Long Life." *New York Times,* April 17, 1990.
"Diet Offers Tantalizing Clues to Long Life." *New York Times,* April 17, 1990.

Bagne, Paul, and Nancy Lucas, "Souls on Ice: Cryoscience." *Omni,* October 1986.

Bailey, John Burn, *Modern Methuselahs.* London: Chapman and Hall, 1888.

Bartholomew, Terese Tse, "Botanical Puns in Chinese Art from the Collection of the Asian Art Museum of San Francisco." *Orientations* (Hong Kong), September 1985.

Bartlett, John, *Familiar Quotations* (11th ed.). Boston: Little, Brown, 1946.

Begg, Paul, "Phantom of the High Seas." *The Unexplained* (London), Vol. 10, Issue 109.

Begley, Sharon, Mary Hager, and Andrew Murr, "The Search for the Fountain of Youth." *Newsweek,* March 5, 1990.

Beil, Laura, "Lean Living." *Science News,* August 27, 1988.

Benet, Sula:
Abkhasians. New York: Holt, Rinehart and Winston, 1974.
How to Live to be 100. New York: Dial Press, 1976.

Booth, William, "Major Longevity Gains Termed Unlikely." *Washington Post,* November 2, 1990.

Bord, Janet, and Colin Bord, *Sacred Waters.* London: Granada, 1985.

"Brain Transplants: A Growing Success." *Science News,* December 20 & 27, 1980.

Brody, Jane E., "The Only Fountain of Youth." *Longevity,* November 1988.

Burkholz, Herbert, "When 'Old' Means Reaching Age 12." *Longevity,* December 1990.

Burtis, C. E., *The Fountain of Youth.* New York: Frederick Fell, 1964.

Carey, John, and Jonathan B. Levine, "More Than an Abortion Drug." *Business Week,* December 17, 1990.

Carpenter, Rhys, and H. M. Herget, "Ancient Rome Brought to Life." *National Geographic,* November 1946.

Carroll, Paul B., "Good News: You Can Live Forever; Bad News: No Sex." *Wall Street Journal,* December 7, 1990.

Carson, Gerald, *The Roguish World of Doctor Brinkley.* New York: Rinehart, 1960.

"Cats: Caressing the Tiger." National Geographic television special. PBS airdate January 9, 1991.

Cavendish, Richard, ed., *Man, Myth & Magic* (Vols. 4, 10, and 11). New York: Marshall Cavendish, 1985.

Cher, and Robert Haas, "Body by Cher." *People,* January 21, 1991.

Cherry, Rona, "Cracking the Code." *Longevity,* July 1989.

"Chill Strikes the Cryonics Business." *Newsweek,* July 7, 1980.

Christie, Anthony, *Chinese Mythology.* New York: Peter Bedrick Books, 1987.

Clarke, Arthur C., *Profiles of the Future.* New York: Warner Books, 1984.

"A Clinically Doggone Beagle." *People,* April 20, 1987.

Cooper, Wendy, *Hair: Sex Society Symbolism.* London: Aldus Books, 1971.

Cornaro, Luigi, *How to Live One Hundred Years.* Wellingborough, England: Thorsons, 1978.

Cramp, Arthur J., *Nostrums and Quackery and Pseudo-Medicine* (Vol. 3). Chicago: American Medical Association, 1936.

Crockett, Arthur, and Timothy Green Beckley, *Count Saint Germain: The New Age Prophet Who Lives Forever*. New Brunswick, N.J.: Inner Light Publications, 1990.

Da Passano, Andrew, and Judith Plowden, *Inner Silence*. San Francisco: Harper & Row, 1987.

Dictionary of Scientific Biography (Vol. 1). New York: Charles Scribner's Sons, 1980.

Dranov, Paula. "Slow Forward." *American Health*, July-August 1989.

Drexler, K. Eric, *Engines of Creation*. New York: Doubleday, 1986.

Elmer-DeWitt, Philip, "You Should Live So Long." *Time*, November 12, 1990.

Ernest, Maurice, *The Longer Life*. London: Adam, 1938.

Ettinger, Robert C. W., *The Prospect of Immortality*. New York: Doubleday, 1964.

Evans, Humphrey, *The Mystery of the Pyramids*. New York: Thomas Y. Cronell, 1979.

"Extending Lifespan with Antioxidants." *Life Extension Report*, August 1987.

Fraser, Cira, "Companion Animals and the Promotion of Health." *Comprehensive Nursing Quarterly*, February 1990.

Fries, James F., and Lawrence M. Crapo, *Vitality and Aging*. San Francisco: W. H. Freeman, 1981.

Frolkis, V. V., *Aging and Life-Prolonging Processes*. Transl. by Nicholas Bobrov. Vienna: Springer-Verlag, 1982.

Gentzel, Mark, "Longevity in China." New York: Black Star, no date.

Georgakas, Dan, *The Methuselah Factors*. New York: Simon and Schuster, 1980.

Gillman, Peter, and Leni Gillman, "Smooth Operators." *The Sunday Times Magazine* (London), July 7, 1991.

Gorney, Cynthia, "Frozen Dreams: A Matter of Death and Life." *Washington Post*, May 1, 1990.

Gray, Asa, *Gray's Manual of Botany*. Ed. by Merritt Lyndon Fernald. New York: D. Van Nostrand, 1970.

Green, Rochelle, "Aging over Thirty: How to Prevent Fifty Percent of It." *Longevity*, June 1989.

Griffith, Lesa, *Help WWF Stop the Rhino Horn Trade*. Campaign report. World Wide Fund for Nature, April 1991.

Harper's Bazaar, January 1991.

Hawkins, Corinne Cullen, "The Cryonic Suspension of Alcor Patient A-1068." *Whole Earth Review*, Fall 1988.

Hayflick, Leonard, "The Cell Biology of Human Aging." *Scientific American*, January 1980.

Heiderer, Tony, "Sacred Space." *National Geographic*, May 1990.

Hershey, Daniel, and Hsuan-Hsien Wang, *A New Age-Scale for Humans*. Lexington, Mass.: Lexington Books, 1980.

Hilton, James, *Lost Horizon*. New York: W. Morrow, 1933.

Holden, Constance, "Why Do Women Live Longer Than Men?" *Science*, October 9, 1987.

Holy Bible (Revised Standard Version). New York: Thomas Nelson & Sons, 1952.

Hyde, Margaret O., and Lawrence E. Hyde, *Cloning and the New Genetics*. Hillside, N.J.: Enslow, 1984.

Ions, Veronica, *Indian Mythology*. New York: Peter Bedrick Books, 1986.

Jeffries, Michael, "Birth on Ice." *Omni*, July 1981.

Kahn, Carol:
"Age-Reversing Drugs." *Longevity*, January 1991.
"An Anti-Aging Aphrodisiac." *Longevity*, December

1990.
Beyond the Helix: DNA and the Quest for Longevity. New York: Times Books, 1985.
"His Theory Is Simple: Eat Less, Live Longer. A Lot Longer." *Longevity*, October 1990.

Kaufmann, Elizabeth, "Fit Forever." *Longevity*, February 1990.

Kent, Saul:
"Interview with Dr. Denham Harman." *Life Extension Report*, August 1987.
"New Lifespan Study with Deprenyl." *Life Extension Report*, November 1990.

Kermis, Marguerite D., *The Psychology of Human Aging*. Boston: Allyn and Bacon, 1984.

King, Francis, "Sex, Sin and Sacrament." *The Unexplained* (London), Vol. 12, Issue 133.

Kneipp, Sebastian, *My Water-Cure*. Transl. by A. de F. Edinburgh: William Blackwood, 1935.

Kohn, Livia, and Yoshinobu Sakade, eds., *Taoist Meditation and Longevity Techniques*. Ann Arbor: University of Michigan, 1989.

Kurtzman, Joel, and Phillip Gordon, *No More Dying: The Conquest of Aging and the Extension of Human Life*. Los Angeles: J. P. Tarcher, 1976.

Lampert, Hope, "Gene Doctoring." *Longevity*, February 1991.

Langone, John, *Long Life*. Boston: Little, Brown, 1978.

Laskas, Jeanne Marie, "Weird Science." *Life*, August 1991.

Lawren, Bill:
"Bionic Body Building." *Longevity*, January 1991.
"A New Piece in the Aging Puzzle." *Longevity*, July 1990.

Leach, Maria, ed., *Funk & Wagnalls Standard Dictionary of Folklore, Mythology and Legend*. San Francisco: Harper & Row, 1984.

Leaf, Alexander:
"Every Day Is a Gift When You Are over 100." *National Geographic*, January 1973.
"Getting Old." *Scientific American*, September 1973.
Youth in Old Age. New York: McGraw-Hill, 1975.

Legeza, Laszlo, *Tao Magic*. London: Thames and Hudson, 1975.

"Le Sacrifice des Kalash." *Géo* (France), no. 35, no date.

Leyel, C. F., *Elixirs of Life*. New York: Samuel Weiser, 1970.

Lin, Robert I-San, *Garlic in Nutrition & Medicine*. Irvine, Calif.: Robert I-San Lin, 1989.

Long, Kim, "When All Else Fails . . ." *Longevity*, June 1989.

McAuliffe, Kathleen, "Live 20 Years Longer, Look 20 Years Younger." *Longevity*, October 1990.

McKinnell, Robert Gilmore, *Cloning of Frogs, Mice, and Other Animals*. Minneapolis: University of Minnesota Press, 1985.

Maclay, Kathleen, "Cryonics Offer Chilly Immortality." *Orange Coast Daily Pilot*, April 18, 1987.

Maranto, Gina, "Aging: Can We Slow the Inevitable?" *Discover*, December 1984.

Marcus, Erin, "Scientists Pinpoint Gene That Shortens Life Span." *Washington Post*, August 24, 1990.

Marsa, Linda, "Cellular Terrorism." *Longevity*, May 1989.

Marti-Ibañez, ed., *The Epic of Medicine*. New York: Clarkson N. Potter, 1962.

Michaud, Sabrina, and Roland Michaud, "Trek to Lofty Hunza—and Beyond." *National Geographic*, November 1975.

Mlot, Christine, "A Well-Rounded Worm.: 220 Kilobases and Counting." *Science*, June 21, 1991.

Morais, Richard C., "Germany's Palm Beach." *Forbes*, April 16, 1990.

Moravec, Hans, *Mind Children*. Cambridge, Mass.: Harvard University Press, 1988.

Morgan, Robert F., and Jane Wilson, *Growing Younger*. Toronto: Methuen, 1982.

Morin, Robert J., ed., *Frontiers in Longevity Research*. Springfield, Ill.: Charles C. Thomas, 1976.

Morrow, Lance, "Ethics: Sparing Parts." *Time*, June 17, 1991.

O'Flaherty, Wendy Doniger (transl.), *Hindu Myths*. London: Penguin Books, 1975.

Oki, Morihiro, *India: Fairs and Festivals*. Tokyo: Gakken, 1989.

Oliver, Jean Duncan, "Resorting to Water." *Health*, April 1990.

Palmore, Erdman B., and Daisaku Maeda, *The Honorable Elders Revisited*. Durham, N.C.: Duke University Press, 1985.

Payer, Lynn, "Rejuvenation Drugs." *Longevity*, June 1989.

Peattie, Donald Culross, *A Natural History of Western Trees*. New York: Crown, 1953.

Perkins, John M., *The Stress-Free Habit*. Rochester, Vt.: Healing Arts Press, 1989.

Pizer, David, and Mike Perry, "Robert Nelson Speaks." *Venturist Monthly News*, August 1990.

Prehoda, Robert W.:
Suspended Animation. New York: Chilton, 1969.

Prentice, Thomson, "Slowing Down the March of Time." *World Press Review*, February 1989.

Rawson, Philip, and Laszlo Legeza, *Tao*. London: Thames and Hudson, 1987.

Reese, Diana, "Reach Out and Heal Someone." *Longevity*, May 1990.

"Reference Guide for a Youthful Face, a Firm Bust, a Toned Body." Brochure. Paris: Clarins, no date.

Reid, Howard, and Michael Croucher, *The Way of the Warrior*. New York: Simon & Schuster, 1987.

Rickard, Bob, "The Holy Incorruptibles." *The Unexplained* (London), Vol. 4, Issue 39.

Roberts, Leslie, "Whatever Happened to the Genetic Map?" *Science*, January 19, 1990.

Rockstein, Morris, and Marvin L. Sussman, eds., *Nutrition, Longevity, and Aging*. Symposium Proceedings. New York: Academic Press, 1976.

Rorvik, David, *In His Image: The Cloning of a Man*. New York: Pocket Books, 1978.

Rosenblum, Gail, "Death by Overwork." *Longevity*, July 1990.

Rosenfeld, Albert:
"Why Women Live Longer Than Men—And How Men Can Start Catching Up." *Longevity*, July 1990.
Prolongevity II. New York: Alfred A. Knopf, 1985.

Roy, P. K., "The Kumbh Conflux." *Frontline* (India), February 4-17, 1989.

Rozek, Michael:
" . . . And Robots Shall Inherit the Earth." *Longevity*, August 1989.
"The Japanese Longevity Diet." *Longevity*, March 1990.

Sanon, Arun, and Gurmeet Thukral, *Festive India*. New Delhi: Frank Bros., 1987.

Sapolsky, Robert M., and Caleb Finch, "On Growing Old." *The Sciences*, March-April 1991.

Schuhmacker, Stephan, and Gert Woerner, eds., *The Encyclopedia of Eastern Philosophy and Religion*. Boston: Shambhala, 1989.

Schulman, Edmund, "Bristlecone Pine, Oldest Known Living Thing." *National Geographic*, March 1958.

Segall, Paul E., and Carol Kahn, *Living Longer, Growing*

Younger. New York: Times Books, 1989.

Segall, Paul E., and Hal Sternberg, ''Rejuvenating the Body and Mind.'' *Life Extension Report,* December 1986.

Segerberg, Osborn, Jr., *The Immortality Factor.* New York: E. P. Dutton, 1974.

Seligmann, Jean, ''For Longer Life, Take a Wife.'' *Newsweek,* November 5, 1990.

Sherman, Carl, and Marie Weaver, ''Eat for Life.'' *Longevity,* September 1990.

Shor, Jean, and Franc Shor, ''At World's End in Hunza.'' *National Geographic,* October 1953.

Shurkin, Joel, ''Longevity Pioneer.'' *Longevity,* April 1989.

Singh, Raghubir, *Ganga: Sacred River of India.* New York: Perennial Press, 1974.

Smolan, Rick, Phillip Moffitt, and Matthew Naythons, *The Power to Heal: Ancient Arts & Modern Medicine.* New York: Prentice Hall Press, 1990.

Storey, Kenneth B., and Janet M. Storey, ''Frozen and Alive.'' *Scientific American,* December 1990.

Tierney, John, ''The Three Secrets of Shangri-la.'' *In Health,* July-August 1990.

Tilak, Shrinivas, *Religion and Aging in the Indian Tradition.* Albany: State University of New York Press, 1989.

Tompkins, Peter, and Christopher Bird, *Secrets of the Soil.* New York: Harper & Row, 1989.

Twombly, Renée, ''Two at a Time.'' *Parents,* September 1990.

''The Ultimate Life Insurance: A Clone.'' *Longevity,* January 1991.

Vogel, Shawna, ''Cold Storage.'' *Discover,* February 1988.

Walford, Roy L.:
Maximum Life Span. New York: W. W. Norton, 1983.
The 120-Year Diet. New York: Simon and Schuster, 1986.

Weidig, Jeffrey C., *A Patient's Guide to Cosmetic Hair Replacement Surgery.* Parker Publications, no date.

Weindruch, Richard, and Roy L. Walford, *The Retardation of Aging and Disease by Dietary Restriction.* Springfield, Ill.: Charles C. Thomas, 1986.

Werner, E. T. C., *Myths & Legends of China.* New York: Benjamin Blom, 1971 (reprint of 1922 edition).

Williams, Gurney, III:
''Resurrection for Sale.'' *Longevity,* May 1989.
''Torpor Treatment.'' *Longevity,* December 1988.

Wolf, Naomi, *The Beauty Myth.* Ed. by James Landis and Elisa Petrini. New York: Morrow, 1991.

Woodhead, Avril D., and Keith H. Thompson, eds., *Evolution of Longevity in Animals.* New York: Plenum Press, 1987.

Wrench, Guy Theodore, *The Wheel of Health.* New York: Schocken Books, 1972 (reprint of 1938 edition).

Yogananda, Paramahansa, *Autobiography of a Yogi.* Los Angeles: Self-Realization Fellowship, 1975.

Young, Stephen, ''A Glimpse of Immortality.'' *New Scientist,* September 15, 1988.

Index

Time-Life Books is a division of Time Life Inc.,
a wholly owned subsidiary of
THE TIME INC. BOOK COMPANY

TIME-LIFE BOOKS

PRESIDENT: Mary N. Davis

Managing Editor: Thomas H. Flaherty
Director of Editorial Resources: Elise D. Ritter-Clough
Director of Photography and Research: John Conrad Weiser
Editorial Board: Dale M. Brown, Roberta Conlan, Laura
Foreman, Lee Hassig, Jim Hicks, Blaine Marshall, Rita
Thievon Mullin, Henry Woodhead
Assistant Director of Editorial Resources/Training Manager:
Norma E. Shaw

PUBLISHER: Robert H. Smith

Associate Publisher: Ann M. Mirabito
Editorial Director: Russell B. Adams, Jr.
Marketing Director: Anne C. Everhart
Production Manager: Prudence G. Harris
Supervisor of Quality Control: James King

Editorial Operations
Production: Celia Beattie
Library: Louise D. Forstall
Computer Composition: Deborah G. Tait (Manager),
Monika D. Thayer, Janet Barnes Syring, Lillian Daniels
Interactive Media Specialist: Patti H. Cass

Library of Congress Cataloging in Publication Data
Search for Immortality / by the editors of Time-Life
Books.
    p. cm.—(Mysteries of the unknown)
    Includes bibliographical references and index.
    ISBN 0-8094-6533-7 (trade)
    ISBN 0-8094-6534-5 (library)
    1. Longevity
    I. Time-Life Books.   II. Series.
    RA776.75.E95 1992
    612.6'8—dc20   91-32277
                                            CIP

MYSTERIES OF THE UNKNOWN

SERIES EDITOR: Jim Hicks
Series Administrator: Jane A. Martin
Art Director: Thomas S. Huestis
Picture Editor: Paula York-Soderlund

Editorial Staff for *Search for Immortality*
Text Editors: Janet Cave (principal), Roberta Conlan
Senior Writer: Esther R. Ferington
Associate Editors/Research: Christian D. Kinney,
Gwen C. Mullen, Sharon Obermiller
Assistant Art Director: Susan M. Gibas
Writer: Sarah D. Ince
Copy Coordinators: Donna Carey, Juli Duncan
Picture Coordinator: Julia Kendrick
Editorial Assistant: Donna Fountain

Special Contributors: Vilasini Balakrishnan (lead research);
Patty U. Chang, Nancy L. Connors, Ann Louise Gates,
Patricia A. Paterno, Evelyn S. Prettyman, Nancy J. Seeger
(research); George Constable, Margery A. duMond, Lydia
Preston Hicks, Harvey S. Loomis, Gina Maranto, Mariah
Burton Nelson, Susan Perry, Peter W. Pocock, Daniel
Stashower (text); John Drummond (design); Hazel
Blumberg-McKee (index).

Correspondents: Elisabeth Kraemer-Singh (Bonn); Christine
Hinze (London); Christina Lieberman (New York); Maria
Vincenza Aloisi (Paris); Ann Natanson (Rome).
Valuable assistance was also provided by Angelika Lem-
mer (Bonn); Nihal Tamraz (Cairo); Barbara Gevene Hertz
(Copenhagen); Robert Kroon (Geneva); Judy Aspinall (Lon-
don); Meenakshi Ganguly (New Delhi); Elizabeth Brown,
Kathryn White (New York); Dag Christensen (Oslo); Ann
Wise, Leonora Dodsworth (Rome); Traudl Lessing
(Vienna).

This volume is one of a series that examines the history
and nature of seemingly paranormal phenomena. Other
books in the series include:

Mystic Places	*Transformations*
Psychic Powers	*Dreams and Dreaming*
The UFO Phenomenon	*Witches and Witchcraft*
Psychic Voyages	*Time and Space*
Phantom Encounters	*Magical Arts*
Visions and Prophecies	*Utopian Visions*
Mysterious Creatures	*Secrets of the Alchemists*
Mind over Matter	*Eastern Mysteries*
Cosmic Connections	*Earth Energies*
Spirit Summonings	*Cosmic Duality*
Ancient Wisdom and Secret Sects	*Mysterious Lands and Peoples*
Hauntings	*The Mind and Beyond*
Powers of Healing	*Mystic Quests*
Search for the Soul	

TIME® LIFE BOOKS